THE BOWERBIRDS

This book is called *Places to Write Home About* because my only criterion for choosing these apartments, lofts, studios and houses is that I like them so much I want to tell other people about them. They are fired by imagination and created by people who refuse to live in a narrowly functional world; they know that creativity and imagination are essential to our lives.

There is something else. The most important future source of historical information about how some people live in New York today is in books like this and certain magazines. In 1848, the great English historian Lord Macaulay wrote, "Readers who take an interest in the progress of civilization and of the useful arts . . . will perhaps wish that historians of far higher pretensions had sometimes spared a few pages from military evolutions and political intrigues, for the purpose of letting us know how the parlors and bedchambers of our ancestors looked."

So here we are, with no pretensions, in the parlors and bedchambers of artists and writers and garden designers, jewellers and professional decorators, photographers and art dealers, architects and fashion editors – in short, the ordinary people of New York – in different niches of the city, who opened up their domestic arrangements to show their ways of living – idiosyncratic, curated, aesthetic, unique, and also spontaneous, unrehearsed and everyday. Their places are never just stationary backdrops – they are provocative presences that elicit interaction, conjured up by people who know that living gracefully does not require attempting the impossible.

In doing this I am merely following in the footsteps of great observers and writers: Mario Praz's masterly *An Illustrated History of Interior Decoration*, published in London in 1964, was both a love letter and a breakthrough in arousing interest in the art of interior decoration. Peter Thornton's *Authentic Decor: The Domestic Interior 1620-1920* (1984) and Charlotte Gere's *Nineteenth-Century Decoration: Art of The Interior* (1989) were seminal. And, of course, the alluring magazine *The World of Interiors*, which first appeared in 1981, was a revelation to many – though, I have to say, my own reaction on seeing it was, "Well! About time too."

Because I grew up in 1950s Northern Ireland, where the decorating ethic in all its fine completeness was Kitchens is Buff and Landings is Brown, where the concept of collecting meant the saving of small pieces of string and brown paper, and where beauty was grimly regarded as an Occasion of Sin, I craved ornament. In *The Merchant of Venice*, that passionate play about the weights and measures of the heart, Bassanio sighs, "The world is still deceived by ornament . . . the guiled shore To a most dangerous sea." Indeed, indeed, and I hoisted my sail and set out on that sea years and years ago and have now lost sight of the shore. But I don't think I've been deceived. I've been delighted and enchanted.

All my adult life I have contrived to live in houses which, crammed with the fruits of my collecting addiction, I think and hope are beautiful – if somewhat disconcerting to any minimalist – and I have always been obsessive about looking at interiors all over the world, and sometimes writing about them. I hold that making your own environment beautiful is as valid a work of art as any piece of writing, or painting or sculpture; we should approach decoration in the way that we approach the other arts. Yet the handiwork, taste, inspiration and labor that goes into composing a pretty room is too often regarded as happenstance. Women have done it throughout the centuries. Edith Wharton wrote about this; she thought of houses and environments as provocative presences and wrote of how decorating her houses and the creativity involved was essential to her, an act of self-definition, a way of finding her voice. (She was a dab hand at description. "The drawing room walls, above their wainscoting of highly varnished mahogany, were hung with salmon-pink damask and adorned with oval portraits of Marie Antoinette and the Princesse de Lamballe. In the center of the florid carpet a gilt table with a top of Mexican onyx sustained a palm in a gilt basket tied with a pink bow. But for this ornament, and a copy of *The Hound of the Baskervilles* which lay beside it, the room showed no traces of human use.")

In this album, I have shown telling examples of the different styles and different ways of living in this tremendous series of towns called New York, a tumbling ziggurat spilling exuberantly across its parks and rivers and neighborhoods. Within the five boroughs are more quartiers and arrondissements than in Paris and more markets and bazaars than in Cairo. There's an infinite diversity of architectural styles and buildings to be seen literally on every side. The inescapable Beaux Arts style, the many monuments by McKim, Mead & White, the white brick 1960s behemoth apartment blocks towering above modest brownstone houses; French gothic chateaux, Italian Renaissance palazzi, sham Louis XVI furbelowed facades flaunt themselves next to restrained Georgian-style town houses; baroque-faced churches, prim Puritan places of worship, elaborate synagogues are jumbled next to turreted fantasies, vast apartment blocks, gleaming mirrored office skyscrapers. It's all utterly New Yorkian. And if, in the great canyons of Manhattan, you look skywards, follies and ornamentation add whimsy to the top of plain-faced buildings, and gardens akin to the fabled Babylonian greenery bloom on the flat roofs of apartment blocks. And, of course, everywhere in Manhattan are those essential icons of the city the water towers – surprisingly vestigial-looking and old-fashioned, and adding greatly to the skyscape.

But looking at New York from the outside gives no clue to its interiors. In *The Decoration of Houses*, those two didactic experts

In the living room of Barbara Jakobson's house on the Upper East Side, the ghost of the Frank Stella wall relief *Felsztyn III* looms over Jeff Koons's *Winter Bears* and the curving "Non-Stop" sofa.

Edith Wharton and architect Ogden Codman Jr insisted that it must never be forgotten that good decoration is interior architecture; but it's an evanescent architecture, and a beautiful interior is so ephemeral, so easily lost, a visual moment gone for ever. Even in families who have lived in houses for generations, the decoration and taste of one era, however inspired, is usually changed, sometimes despised by the next. (I remember at auction a gilded bureau inlaid with mother-of-pearl and tortoiseshell by Boulle, the great French court cabinetmaker of the seventeenth century. Surely no one who saw it could fail to be bowled over by its exquisite if overwrought beauty. Yet it had lain in a dusty attic for over a hundred years. It sold in 1988 for £1.2 million.) Given the perpetual work-in-progress and ruthless remaking of New York, where so little is permanent or revered, the restoration of the Payne Whitney house (now the offices of the Cultural Services of the French Embassy) on Fifth Avenue is an almost-miracle.

In writing about contemporary decoration, trying to grasp the essence of a current period is important. And almost impossible. In *Authentic Decor* Peter Thornton wrote, "What characterizes a period in the field of interior decoration is the density of pattern and arrangement that prevails at the time." But there is no discernible inclusive density of pattern and arrangement in my chosen places. Some are penny plain and some are tupenny colored. Some are the homes of architects. Linda Pollak and Sandro Marpillero transformed a nineteenth-century shoe factory into a live-work loft. Bastien Halard was his own architect in recovering their house from dingy apartments to the clarity it has now. Others have used architects to orchestrate their ideas and plans: the architect Sam White, great-grandson of Stanford White of McKim, Mead & White, played a major role in the early stages of restoring James Fenton's Harlem house; Gordon VeneKlasen had the architect Annabelle Selldorf design the major turnaround in his mews house. Some are the homes of decorators, and others have used decorators. But all are in essence the creation of their owners.

Many of the owners — writers, poets, artists, creators, and image bandits — are collectors; not one is a passive consumer. Collecting is a problematic subject. It's often deciphered as being related to a stifled creative urge, and one plausible theory is that collecting is not only an instrument designed to allay a basic need but also an escape hatch for feelings of danger and the re-experience of loss. Yet, for all the evidence of a collecting habit, nothing seems perceptibly stifled about these rooms full of idiosyncrasies and comfort in every sense; certainly, they reveal the affection the owners have for objects and paintings and their careful placement often results in a witty piece of domestic theater.

The arrangements in many of these rooms show the intuitive and exacting discipline these collectors bring to bear on their habit. Saul Bellow said that culture means having access to your own soul and these rooms are full of culture and soul (though none, praise be, are soulful: they may be conceived as a mirror of the spirit but there's a fair bit of irony scattered around). As *Vogue* scolded in a 1925 article on decoration: "We shall find any interior that does not flow from our own instincts a cold unconvincing background for ourselves."

Sometimes when writing about the owners and their rooms my mind strayed to the habits of the bowerbird, that great master of delightful, transient installation in the natural world. He — yes, he — constructs elaborate bowers and tunnels adorned with pebbles, feathers, shells, bits of glass, "not as nests," the dictionary says, "but as places of resort." (But then again, the bowerbird is among the most behaviorally complex of bird species.)

As we see, so we are — that is a grade of human character, connected to the quality of perception of the external world. William Morris's famous and kindly advice holds as true today as when he issued it nearly 150 years ago: "If you want a golden rule that will fit everything, this is it: Have nothing in your houses that you do not know to be useful or believe to be beautiful."

I'm chary of pronouncing on questions of taste — one person's taste is often another's opportunity for eye-rolling — but I'm not chary of pronouncing on what makes a house a beautiful place to live in and to be looked at, regardless of size, period or proportions. Such houses contain spaces that are rational and are full of personal vision, often calm, with the power to affect feelings.

Being in these places can lighten the heart — and, what's more, looking around them is an educative process. Some here are a brilliant curation of the art of the twentieth and the twenty-first centuries; another has examples of work from the American Arts and Crafts epoch; here is early Peruvian religious imagery; and there is a rare example of the art of the Mound Builders, one of the vanished cultures of North America. All are lessons to the eye.

There's a touching and cringe-making sequence in *Swann's Way* concerning Odette, the beautiful, sly and stupid courtesan who professes to be deeply interested in furniture. Swann, one of Proust's saddest and most lovable characters, a gentleman, elegant, intellectual, with refined taste (and enormously rich) allows himself to be debased by his obsessive love for her. When he mildly criticizes her friend for buying a job lot of pretentious sham-antique furniture, she blurts out to Swann what she really thinks of his own (exquisite, understated) house: "You wouldn't have her live like you, among a lot of broken-down chairs and threadbare carpets!"

There's no sham among these things here, and there are some threadbare carpets. And I warrant Odette wouldn't have been overly keen on Kenneth Lane's dishtowel cushions or Jane Rosenblum's anaglyptic staircase.

The way we arrange our house interiors is an advertisement for our interior life. Emotional disharmony makes for disturbing and untidy and even slovenly environments; and places have profound effects on well-being, and style and taste are like perfect manners.

On this showing New York is full of balanced, wise, deeply clean, perceptive and enchanting people, who use their personality traits and imagination to the fullest. The one thing all these paragons share is that they love their home town with a passion. John Updike summed it up: "The true New Yorker secretly believes that people living anywhere else have to be, in some sense, kidding."

So, these are letters about places of resort to write home about, to the misguided people who live elsewhere; and, of course, they are love letters.

OPPOSITE Timothy Van Dam and Ron Wagner's Orientalist Library in Harlem.
PAGES 10–11 Matelots, windswept maidens, shells and patterns in rich purples, reds and yellows frolic over a 1936 *verre églomisé* cabinet. It comes from the Helena Rubinstein estate and now is in Amy Fine Collins's Upper East Side dining room.

Here we are

INCANDESCATION

JANE ROSENBLUM

When I first met the artist Jane Kaplowitz, aka Jane Rosenblum, walking up the street with her dog, her black hair in an aureole around her vivid face, I thought her house might look the way it looks — except the reality is mega times better. She has taken the work of other artists and made a single creation (unlike some, who use their houses as backdrop for their own art — and none the worse for that).

She lives in a brownstone on West 10th Street (a street included in a map of Women's Rights Historic Sites) and as I climb the stoop, with trees in pots on either side, a photographer is taking shots of her house. "So pretty," she murmurs. Nearby hangs a blue plaque commemorating Emma Lazarus, who wrote the poem "The New Colossus," to help raise money

for that symbol of the United States the Statue of Liberty. The last lines are engraved on the statue:

Send these, the homeless, tempest-tossed to me,
I lift my lamp beside the golden door!

To enter Jane's house is to step inside the golden door and be walloped by a Technicolor spectacle full of strange things, like a fabulous turn-of-the-century bazaar as imagined, say, by Balzac high on opium — that is until you look at the paintings and then you are, wham-bang, catapulted into an echt contemporary, almost a distillation of eclectic New York art of the last few decades.

PAGES 12–13 Above the original marble fireplace in the sitting room is a painting by Alex Hay, partly framed by peacock feathers in some of Jane's collection of Italian urns. To the left is a drawing of Gilbert (of Gilbert and George) by George above a drawing by Terry Winters; to the right, a painting by Christopher Brooks. ABOVE In a corner of the sitting room is a papier mâché sculpture by Theo Rosenblum. Behind, to its right, is an abstract by Peter Halley. OPPOSITE CLOCKWISE FROM TOP LEFT Under a glimpse of Joshua Reynolds's painting of *Venus and Cupid*, the dining room mantelpiece holds a photograph of the Queen Mother and an ice cream cone figure by Theo Rosenblum. At the end of the hallway, lined with paintings, Jane's rescue dog Cloud guards the door. A sculpture shark by Theo Rosenblum. In a corner of Jane's studio a series of drawings reveals her passion for dogs.

There is more to Jane than meets the eye and that's saying a lot. Her interiors and arrangements are anarchic, sophisticated events and a clever hang. There is also a sense of mutual admiration and kinship with other artists; by way of being a testament to how much her artist friends love her. Often when I inquire about the provenance of a piece or ask: "Where did you get that?" she slightly blushes (only slightly, mind) – and it transpires it was made by a friend and/or given by a friend. Friends tell loving stories about her – if I mention how wonderfully jam-packed her apartment is, I'm told, "You should have seen it before. What you are seeing now is Jane's version of minimalism."

She is a witty social commentator on the art scene, and there is a mordant humor, of a paradoxical "you couldn't make it up" quality in many of the paintings and objects here. On one wall alone one can do a quick canter through a significant section of recent East Coast art movements. A big abstract by Peter Halley jostles for space with a papier mâché life-size figure, a cross between a caveman and a shaman, by Jane's son, the artist Theo Rosenblum, near to a Gilbert and George piece. All this in turn alongside flea market finds with their own terrible and idiosyncratic charm. "That house on 10th Street," a friend said fondly, is "kind of awful and wonderful at the same time." Aweful would be a better word, if it existed.

The interior of the innocuous brownstone arrives to my eyes from somewhere beyond my experience of houses. Each room springs its own surprises. Paintings and objects line every room and corridor from the skirting boards to gilt spray-painted elaborate cornices. Plus, you would be well advised to keep your head down here. Chandeliers reign: one with elaborately festooned ruby glass, another sporting multicolored Chinese bulbs from the Bowery, another from a hotel in Miami. Above the red sofa, with its multiplicity of leopard-patterned cushions, is a huge painting by David McDermott and Peter McGough called, unequivocally, *Cocksucker*. "It's not like their usual work," she murmurs.

So the house is a tumultuous artwork in itself, romantically expressed, a work of creative imagination, with abrupt declarative bursts of color – but then Jane has been an artist all her life, and her work is shown at many galleries and museums. In 2004 she joined Yale University School of Art as a critic in painting and printmaking in Manhattan. She became a collector and a reluctant dealer ("I hate selling things but I do") after she married the celebrated, erudite and irreverent writer, art critic and professor Robert Rosenblum in 1977. They shared a passion for, to put it simply, Art. "He already was buying art so then we started buying it together." He died in 2006.

Twenty-five years ago they bought this brownstone in Greenwich Village and turned it into the joyous and important place it is today. Before that they lived in an apartment with a doorman (she shudders) in Mercer Street. "I hated the whole feel of that place and I'd always liked the idea of living in a house," she says, "and when we started searching, Robert, who was then teaching at NYU, drew a circle around where he wanted to live so he could walk to work. We saw this house, didn't like it and went away on holiday and when we came back we said, 'Let's look again.' It was terrible – oh, well beyond terrible. It had belonged to the painter Luigi Lucioni, and he had divided it into apartments for his sisters Alice and Aurora. They lived here during the winter for many decades and after they died Luigi divided it again, into eight apartments. Cookers everywhere – it was a huge rehab job. Huge. And even after we moved in it took me a long while to like it. It was such a big change, I couldn't deal with it." (Her children – Theo, and daughter Sophie, a writer – were aged seven and nine when they made the radical move.)

Her house is an extension of her character, her way of looking and seeing, and her temperament. The rooms may be crammed with paintings, books, objects and idiosyncratic furniture but, inadvertent as it seems, there is rhyme and reason to the installation, not just as a narrative of their singular married life but also as a place that mediates between various genres of art and various hierarchies. She's kernel code, is Jane.

Some pieces came from shops long since vanished from SoHo (and she is one of many artists who mourn the passing of the old shops and flea market). But she ranges far afield for her acquisitions. In the dining room a Miami chandelier hangs above a crashed glass table by the French artist Daniel Clément, who makes spectacular pieces for the label Les Meubles Précieux. (She brought it over from Paris. "The shipping!" she whispers to herself, staring at the extremely heavy table. "The shipping!")

The table bids to dominate the dining room, but is outfaced at every turn. A mirrored Plexiglas piece by Kelley Walker fills one wall, near a vivid work from the 1980s by Frank Stella, hanging below a collage by Bruce Conner. The copper chairs are made by Blue Dot, a Minneapolis-based modern furniture company, and, startlingly enough, the painting over the mantelpiece that looks like a Joshua Reynolds *is* a Joshua Reynolds. *Venus and Cupid*. Well, I never! (But then again there's a Francis Danby in the hall.) Underneath the Reynolds a photograph of the Queen Mother is propped next to a slightly obscene plaster ice cream cone by Theo. In a corner is a screen by McDermott and McGough and a Charles Shaw shaped canvas.

A disturbing painting by the metaphysical realist Alan Turner, of planes of flesh, close-ups of body parts and a single almost Cyclopic eye, fills the wall above one of the brilliant green cabinets with their crossed spears, on which roost many stuffed birds – not to mention an ivory articulated grasshopper.

In the sitting room, with its handsome windows flooding the room with light, is a marble curved fireplace, its mantelpiece crammed with urn-shaped, eye-wateringly colored Italian vases found in a junk shop in Bellport featuring scenic (very) views of classical temples ("cuckoo pots," Jane calls them), peacock feathers and diverse ferocious objects. Below there's a yellow tole faux bamboo table that wouldn't be out of place in

PAGES 16–17 The crushed glass dining room table is by Daniel Clément. Above it hangs a chandelier Jane found in Miami. The painting on the left of the fireplace is by Alan Turner and on the right a work by Frank Stella hangs below a collage by Bruce Conner. On the wall to the right is a vast piece by Kelley Walker. OPPOSITE In the light-filled sitting room, a Chairman Mao cushion, made by Jane, looks at a yellow Regency-style tole table on a rug by Laurie Simmons. On the table is a little ceramic vase by Elisabeth Kley, and in front of the left-hand window is a sculpture by Klara Lidén. Above is a painted glass bulb chandelier, found in the Bowery.

Party Dress

an English Regency house, bearing other intriguing objects, including an exuberant cylinder by the art writer and ceramicist Elisabeth Kley and two stuffed ravens being stuffed ravens (part of the flock of taxidermy in the apartment) perched on a Laurie Simmons rug featuring a person in a pink tutu leaping beyond kitsch into the blue. This genteel table is overlooked by a large drawing of George of Gilbert and George, which in turn hangs above a beautiful drawing by Terry Winters. A large stuffed goose is perched nearby. I question it. Jane explains patiently: "The goose is a goose."

Beside the fireplace is an asphalt and wood creation by Klara Lidén. "Great young artist," Jane also explains. A minimalist painting by Alex Hay hangs near a painting by the English artist Christopher Brooks, overlooking an elegant canapé sporting many cushions, the one of Chairman Mao made by Jane herself. Cultural revolution springs to mind. She has a sly sense of humor and a wit that often makes you do a double take. On the window wall is a painting by Beatrice Wood (better known as a ceramic artist) with, below, a painting of a sort of cow by Alex Katz: "He isn't known for his cows," says Jane, "except for some of the women he paints." A large abstract by Peter Halley is juxtaposed with a painting by the often transgressive African-American Robert Colescott, this one typical of his exuberant, comical, often bitter reflections and fantasias on interracial romance, race and situation; it hangs above the painting *Jack the Ripper*, an example of appropriation art, as practiced by Mike Bidlo, one of a series titled *Not Pollock*, using the same materials and media as Jackson Pollock.

Images of dogs abound – Jane's husband's love for their bulldog, Archie, inspired him to write *The Dog in Art: From Rococo to Post-Modernism*. There's a model of a disenchanted sunglass-wearing pug with images in the lens – another gift from a friend, Mayer Rus, an editor on *Architectural Digest*. A real live dog, Cloud, a rescue, snoozies around.

This extraordinary woman, Jane Kaplowitz, was born in New York State: "My parents were Polish/Russian and I grew up in a place beyond beyond, and beyond that again, in Canarsie, in the outer reaches of Brooklyn. It's now called aspirational. My mother worked all hours God sends, but she made time to take me to look at things in museums, and after a while I realized I was far more interested in the actual refined beautiful spaces of the museums and galleries than the art on the walls. It was always the space that attracted me."

She went to the Pratt Institute "as a fashion person," but a seminal moment occurred when, after six months, she visited a de Kooning exhibition. She was overwhelmed by what she saw and experienced. It was an epiphany about art and about her life. "I thought, 'What I am doing at Pratt?'" Well, she graduated and then transferred to the Art Institute of Chicago. A performance by the radical dancer and filmmaker Yvonne Rainer brought about another change in her not quite chosen way of life. She was blown away by how Rainer integrated the everyday of movements of life into art. "This is art?" Rainer's work is a continuing inspiration. Her own work has an intimate connection to her daily life and is entwined with

In the kitchen *Party Dress*, a painting by Steve Gianakos, hangs over a toile- and cushion-covered banquette. The cupboards are fronted with scarlet Formica.

the happenings and events and people — so many of them artists — in that busy and sociable life. She is a fine draftswoman, emotionally driven, with an extraordinary sense of color and her own rare vision.

Underneath the public exhibition she is a private person. It's not easy to gain access to her studio, up the startling staircase with its exuberant raised circles in gilt on vivid green. ("The house-painters picked them out.") Above the dado, on a pink background, are even more pictures, including one by Luis Meléndez, next to an irreverent drawing of *Big Lonely Queens* by the fabulous drag artist Taboo. (Cecil Beaton is in there, and William Burroughs, and a dozen other notables.)

Her studio is worth seeing. A wall of windows overlooks a narrow iron balcony covered with wisteria looking over the trees in the gardens of neighboring houses. The big room is an alluring bravura mess, the walls looking like drip paintings in themselves, with a series of blurred but perfect drawings of the same dog pinned above stacks of plastic beakers for paint-mixing. A postcard reading I HATE NEW YORK is tipsily pinned up among other ephemera.

She is a true bohemian, unselfconscious in her aesthetic freedom, her liberalities, and her delight in the world at large; her littered house embodies that spirit which Italians call *buttato lì* — artful artfulness.

OPPOSITE In the hallway, a cluster of typically idiosyncratic objects sit above the radiator, below a Francis Danby landscape. Above, to the right, is a still life by Luis Meléndez. The raised patterns below the dado are original, as is all the plasterwork. They were picked out and painted by Jane's house-painters. ABOVE LEFT A beaded curtain is decorated with the image of Jacques-Louis David's *Napoleon Crossing the Alps*. Above it is a serigraph by Jim Richard. ABOVE RIGHT A papier mâché sculpture by Theo Rosenblum.

A GARDEN IN BROOKLYN

MIRANDA BROOKS & BASTIEN HALARD

As I walked to Miranda Brooks and Bastien Halard's house in Brooklyn a man was vacuum-cleaning the street outside? As it transpires, it had nothing to do with Miranda's household arrangements, but I wouldn't have been at all surprised if it had, as her four-story brownstone with its "humble elegance" (in John Fowler's famous phrase) is immaculate.

Everything about and around Miranda Brooks is good-looking, including her house, her children and her French architect husband. Well, good-looking is an understatement. Banked-up beautiful would be more accurate.

She has been practicing as a landscape architect and garden designer since 1991 (Miranda Brooks Landscape Design) and is a contributing editor to *Vogue*. She runs her practice out of the pretty carriage house at the back of the house across the garden, planted with glorious abundance so that you thread your way through greenery and color to reach the offices where her garden designers work.

She may seem coolness itself, but she is an inspired garden designer and gets under the skin of the gardens she makes. If you analyzed her character from her gardens she is not at all cool, but passionate, voluptuous, lavish, abundant, and often grand, without ever being too formal. She has a subtle, painterly approach laid over strict underlying design. It may all seem spontaneous, romantic, pastoral, but she keeps any plant making a run for it on a tight rein. Practical aspects are priorities. Cut paths may meander freely through whispering long grass – but that grass doesn't get overgrown.

A knowledgeable plantswoman, she also has a percipient eye for landscape and perspective and is able to visualize the long-term result of her planting. Her gardens are to be lived in, not just looked at. The artist and cleric William Gilpin wrote in a letter in 1769, "I have had a dispute lately – on an absurd vulgar opinion which holds that we see with our eyes whereas I assent that our eyes are only mere glass windows and we see with our imagination." This Miranda does. For example, the bewitching series of mature secret gardens for Anna Wintour that have evolved under her care over twenty years reveals a rampant visual imagination. She tells me that someone once said to her about gardening: "It's an awful profession in a way . . . It's like being an interior decorator whose furniture dies." Though she laughs, she agrees. "You do really have to love it to do it."

She learned to love it when she was made to work in the garden after school in the evenings for a year at her parents' farm in Hertfordshire, as a punishment. For? "For doing something terrible!" Far from its being a penance, she immediately knew this was to be something special in her life. She took a degree in art history at the Courtauld Institute of Art, a postgraduate degree in landscape architecture at the University of Birmingham, and then worked for that doyenne of garden designers Arabella Lennox-Boyd, before starting out on her own.

The house is in Boerum Hill, opposite a basketball stadium and a social housing project. The area was snidely described in the *New York Times* as "the aspirational space of the year . . . an idealized backdrop for the chattering classes . . . here are all the trappings of the suburban good life and the attendant complexities."

Be that as it may, there is nothing suburban about Miranda and Bastien's international bohemian house; but it was far from that when they found it on Craigslist. As soon as Bastien clapped eyes on it he called Miranda to tell her not to bother to make the journey from Manhattan: "It won't do, the garden is too small . . . It's opposite the projects." But she and her brother Sebastian had already started out and when she saw the pretty carriage house at the bottom of the garden – though it wasn't a garden then, covered as it was in solid paving stones – the deal was clinched. Now, far from disliking the projects opposite, she would rather have their open playing spaces opposite her house than other buildings. "It gives us complete privacy," she says, "though sometimes when a game is on the children can hear some pretty choice language floating up!"

There was a lot to do before they could move in: the main house was divided into multiple dwellings and the entry passage to the house behind ran right through it. "The conversion only took eight months," Miranda says, "and I don't know how Bastien did it. But it was urgent. We had two-year-old Poppy and Grey was a baby and we simply had no room in the house where we were living."

Her husband, being a sympathetic architect with strict ideas about how he likes houses to look, knew just what to do. His wide knowledge of furniture, architecture and decoration was imbued in him in what sounds like a gorgeously creative childhood in France. His great-grandfather Adolphe Halard founded Nobilis, the French fabric and wallpaper company; his grandfather Yves Halard, and his wife, the decorator Michelle Halard, started their own interior design firm. Nowhere much to run with that background – although run he did, and fetched up in New York, where he met Miranda at a dinner party and that was that. She's got a pretty good design pool too. Her father is an architect and a don at Cambridge and her mother, a psychologist, lives with her dogs in Colorado ("a very cool exterior hiding a deeply romantic interior," says Miranda).

"The least expensive way of making something nice is to keep the charm of it," Bastien says. He hates fake traditional. He preserved the staircase, exposed the ceiling joists downstairs to give height, and designed and built a lot of the furniture in the house. And, of course, both of them have oodles of that dreaded quality, taste. It wasn't all easy going. Miranda says, "Our builders worked on it without much reading of plans."

"Oh, they read plans," Bastien says, "but sometimes they read them upside down. Once when I arrived they had erected a pillar not only in the wrong room but also upside down."

Miranda did all the colors in the house. She bought the paint from the wondrous Papers and Paints shop in London's Fulham

Shaded by a crab apple tree, the pretty carriage house at the end of the garden is where Miranda has her offices.

Road, and discovered how different New York light is from English light. "Unbelievably so. The pale green willow walls in the girls' bathroom turned into a dark green, and the whites just looked gloomy." No evidence here – this house is luminous.

One can see that the interior is a result of a combination of unusual factors . . . Miranda's very English sensibility, Bastien's cosmopolitan Frenchness, their lives as New Yorkers, their two different businesses, and their growing children. So, two designers doing the same house? How did that play out?

"There was a certain amount of argument," she says, dryly, "so we designated floors. The French could win arguments on the first floor, the English got to win on the children's floor, and the combination of the two made it easier on the top floor, where the bathroom doubles as a library and sitting room. Yes, there were disagreements – whether the loo should be in the bathroom or in a small back room blocking the light. Bastien,

being French, wanted the small dark room." There isn't a small dark room.

It's a lovely bathroom, conducive to relaxation and chat, and they spend time up here in the evening after work. An eighteenth-century Swedish carved bench was Miranda's first buy at auction and Bastien built the bookshelves and painted the tub a deep blue to match the indigo curtains (dyed by Miranda). A Gerrit Rietveld pendant light much loved by Bastien hangs above.

Their adjacent bedroom, through the dressing room past an ottoman covered in a Japanese *boro*, is a pastoral dream rimmed with light, a crab apple tree knocking at the window. The looking glass over the fireplace opposite the bed was found in a flea market, and the bed is big. Big. Bastien carved its headboard from a solid maple tree trunk; behind it a panoramic stretch of De Gournay "Tree of Life" wallpaper echoes the flowery spread of the crab apple.

ABOVE In the airy sitting room with its high exposed-joist ceiling, pictures cover the walls. To the left of the fireplace mirror is a photograph by François Halard; to the right, from left, a photograph by Adam Fuss above a painting by Simone Shubuck, two pictures by Christopher Brooks, and a portrait by Dan McCarthy. The modern chair and table were made by Bastien.
OPPOSITE Bastien also designed and made the couple's bed, which they wanted, says Miranda, to be vast enough "to fit everyone." Behind, in the custom-made De Gournay "Tree of Life" wallpaper, doves nestle in the branches as they do in the garden outside.

The second floor is devoted to the children's room – and this house is filled with children and their accoutrements: gleanings of their drawings lie on a kitchen table next to muffins baked by Poppy (delicious). The wall-sized notice board in the central playroom is covered in their artistic efforts, and their bedrooms are rural retreats papered with hand-blocked lino prints by the London-based artist Marthe Armitage – chestnut trees for Grey, and a mingling of images of butterflies, birds and cobwebs for Poppy. This place is full of creativity – cooking, dancing, dressing up, painting, planning.

Much of it takes place in the kitchen, a long room, stretching from the windows overlooking the street to the view over the luxuriant garden behind. There's a nacreous gleam to it, an effect heightened by the limed beamed ceiling and the limed floor of white oak, giving it a Provençal air. The countertop, nearly 40 feet long, is also made from old white oak and above it hangs a buoyant gallery of paintings and drawings, a kind of anthology of work done by friends, including paintings by Christopher Brooks (Miranda's ex-husband), drawings by their friend Dan McCarthy and by their neighbors Elliott Puckette and Hugo Guinness and photographs by Adam Fuss, another friend. The watercolors are by the gifted botanical artist Emma Tennant, who grew up at Chatsworth and has written, "I cannot remember

a time when I was not interested in both gardening and painting. I must have been born with a trowel in one hand and a paintbrush in the other" – which sounds very like Miranda.

In the middle of the room a drowsy Beldi keep tabs on the activity – no hint that she was rescued as a starving puppy found in Morocco, and that to get her here involved a Byzantine journey via Egypt. She lives in peace with the girls' cats, Caliban and Tempette.

The glory of the house is what Miranda has created on her rooftop – a proper garden, with a pergola and a vegetable plot, rampant with lettuce and carrots and a little bothy like something out of a fairy tale where the family and friends had candlelit suppers on balmy Brooklyn nights among the garden scents. But a snitchy neighbor informed the planning people of the little hidden shack, and they had to remove it. As soon as they get planning permission back up it goes, a labor of love. The girls have a quadrant of garden up there and they harvest the vegetables they have planted and tended.

They have fantasies about buying the house next door and extending laterally so that everything is twice the size it is now. "It's a complete fantasy," Miranda says. "This is the best family house. You hear coming down the stairwell the sound of children laughing, your work people are straight across the garden. If I were asked to describe it? I would say it is a happy house."

ABOVE The children's artwork covers one whole wall in the open, colorful playroom. A vase filled with anemones sits on the low playroom table, made by Bastien, whose shelves are full of coloring books. OPPOSITE, CLOCKWISE FROM TOP LEFT On the left of the bathroom's central window is a portrait by Dan McCarthy; on the right, a photograph by Mark Borthwick above a drawing by Hugo Guinness; the iconic hanging light is by Gerrit Rietveld. On the mantelpiece in the main bedroom are a drawing by Emma Tennant and a Russian icon of St Nicholas. Caliban, the ragdoll cat, descends the original, reclaimed staircase. In Poppy's bedroom, wallpaper hand-blocked with butterflies, birds and cobwebs.

A SUBSTANTIAL WORLD

DONALD & PATRICIA ORESMAN

Some apartments in New York are startling on first impact. One such stunner is in a duplex in the Gainsborough Studios, a Landmark slender building erected in 1908 to the design of Charles W. Buckham on Central Park South near Columbus Circle, which has been beautifully restored with its facade of vivid geometric tiles and Gothic-style window screens. It speaks of a different world from the brazen bleak brass and black Trump tower nearby.

So. Once inside the cast-iron door you're in a foyer with Arts and Crafts charm, warm red polished tiles on the floor, an eccentric elevator. The building was commissioned by a group of artists to provide comfortable artistic quarters - 18-foot-high studios and double-height windows to let in the northern light. Those windows have a magnificent view looking due north over Central Park and on a sunny day it looks like Utopia out there. But then again everything up here is fairly wonderlandish.

The elevator doors open, you pass through an ordinary door and you achieve metaphoric lift. I wouldn't be surprised if I'd tumbled down a hole into this little conceit, a pied-à-terre fitted out as a Renaissance-style library of polished French maple wood, compact, detailed, with pediment-topped and pilaster-detailed bookcases, a coffered ceiling and a mezzanine-level gallery. It's a retreat for living and reading and dreaming where physical details and metaphysical ideas interact in an enclosed world and it's the achieved dream space of a successful and formidable man, one who couldn't have looked and behaved in a more ordinary and more businesslike way. His name was Donald Oresman and for years he was a highly successful attorney, general counsel of Paramount Communications and member of the board of more philanthropic organizations than one would care to count. He was also a visionary, a committed conservationist (chairman of New York Landmarks Conservancy), and he was passionate about the arts and especially about literature. Reading was his pleasure and escape and he felt as one with George Steiner — whom he often quoted — about the profoundly solitary and fierce privacy in the act of reading.

Donald Oresman also loved looking at things. He shared both these pursuits with his wife, Patricia, another avid reader, whom he had married in 1948 ("the smartest decision of my life"). Together they began to amass their treasury of books and later to buy twentieth-century images — with this twist: every single one, from everywhere and in all styles in every conceivable medium, oil paintings, prints, drawings, photographs, watercolors, acrylics, needlepoint, painted leather, gouaches and ceramics; sculptures, in bronze, cast iron, balsa wood, in marble, in stone, in wood, papier mâché, glass, scrap metal and polyadam (a delightful pair of bookends by Tom Otterness) — all had to be on subject of people in the act of reading. He was relentless in his pursuit. "There's a bit of the Captain Ahab about me," he admitted cheerily.

This double-height library was designed to house at least two thousand books —mostly literary criticism, contemporary fiction and poetry — and

Elegantly carved maple wood creates stairs, galleries, bookshelves and a series of enticing reading spaces around a central light-filled sitting area. The angled oil painting behind the sofa is *Counting Sheep* by Katherine Freeman.

much the same number of works of art. But the art collection was forever expanding. "I think I built it too small," he mourned, but he knew there had to be a limit. Not that he ever reached it.

The collection is 95 per cent North American or European; the rest is from South America and Japan. He had his favorite eras, the 1920s, 1930s and 1940s, and he particularly liked the work of the early twentieth-century Ashcan School. It's a catholic assemblage and now includes – let's do this alphabetically and geographically – examples by Balthus, Aubrey Beardsley, Max Beerbohm, Vanessa Bell, Chagall, Cocteau, Roger Fry, Alberto Giacometti, Eric Gill, Duncan Grant, Gwen John, Fernand Léger, Magritte, Matisse, Henry Moore, Picasso and Diego Rivera; American artists include Thomas Hart Benton, Abe Blashko, Elizabeth Catlett, Richard Diebenkorn, Jim Dine, Doris Lee, Reginald Marsh, Larry Rivers, David Smith, Tabitha Vevers and Andy Warhol.

Everything here has strength of personality or presence; it's been scrutinized before being allowed in. Oresman was somewhat dismissive of photographs. "They have to be fairly adventurous to interest me," he said. "Otherwise they're verging on journalism." (Paradoxically, Robert Henri, the leader of that ragbag company of New York artists the Ashcan School, specifically wanted art to be akin to journalism.) Nevertheless, Oresman owned photographs by such great names as Berenice Abbott, Henri Cartier-Bresson and Robert Frank. But *au fond*

he didn't care about names – it was how the artist viewed the subject. "There is an intensity to reading that captures artists' imaginations," he said, "a very private element to it."

It all started when he and his wife bought a 1973 lithograph by Jim Dine called *Nancy Reading*, published by the remarkable Petersburg Press. A few weeks later they bought a drawing by Larry Rivers of the poet Frank O'Hara, nose in a book, and that was that. In the face of the evidence piled around him, the vast accumulation, he was happily adamant that he wasn't a collector and indeed was bemused as to why I burst into laughter. "I'm orderly," he protested, "so we decided we would concentrate on one area." "Have it your own way, Donald," I said in familiar fashion, "but you're a dyed-in-the-wool, hard-core, chronic, incorruptible collector." He had the grace to laugh, but continued in full-scale denial. "I am not a collector and I am not interested in books as objects." We left it at that.

"I have a clerical mind," he said, "and I follow a rigorous policy. If I buy something framed, I hang it on the wall, and if I buy something unframed I stick it under the bed." Well, I suppose under the bed is one way of describing the meticulously designed maze of drawers filled with drawings pleated into every available inch of the library. Other works are stored in complex double and triple layered sets of intricately constructed sliding and hinged panels that swing open to reveal pictures on pictures – like the Hogarthian sets in Sir John Soane's Museum in London.

OPPOSITE Huge north-facing windows look out across Central Park. Mounted on the pedimented mirror is Michael Hurson's *Study for Man Reading Newspaper*; among the paintings lined up on the floor are *Woman and Literature – Medina and Gillian*, by Claire Khalil, and *The Deaf Man Heard the Dumb Man Say That the Blind Man Saw the Lame Man*, by Michael Lenson. ABOVE The library accommodates a charming dining area. The mahogany and leather table is a reproduction of a Victorian one Donald Oresman liked.

He knew exactly what he wanted when he commissioned the interior design of the apartment in 1996. He gave free rein to his architect, Richard Sammons of Fairfax & Sammons, with one proviso. "I told I him didn't want it to be dark wood – mahogany, heavy – I wanted it to be light and airy and it needed to be practical and comfortable because I wanted to live here too during the week, to eat, sleep – and read." (In the country house in Larchmont he had over ten thousand books and there is an Oresman Gallery in the local library.)

So this library doubles discreetly as a living room with a fireplace and a dining room, and behind a door at the back, a bedroom and a bathroom.

When he bought the apartment it had white walls and many mirrors; the big window with its architrave filling the north wall was already there. "The place was awful," the architect remembered, "like a racquetball court." It took about nine months to remodel it and the result is this light-filled confection with a series of bookcases projecting out at right angles, making shadowy reading spaces within each bay. The gleaming surfaces are carefully articulated, and the shelves have pediment facades modelled on ancient tabernacles where scrolls were kept. The fireplace in the central bay has a *trompe l'œil* timber chimneypiece painted black to resemble marble, and on its hearthstone Samuel Beckett's famous mantra "Try again, Fail again, Fail better" was carved by the English master carver Simon Verity. Above this level is the curved mezzanine gallery

housing more books and pictures and the balustraded bed space balcony flanked by bowed mirrored cupboard doors giving different views and perspectives. It's reached by a precipitous spiral staircase, based on the helix-shaped one in the Loretto Chapel in Santa Fe, known as the Miraculous Stair.

Every year at Christmas Donald Oresman and his wife sent their friends a delicious little bon-bon of a book privately printed and usually illustrated by his great friend Brendan Gill of the *New Yorker*. The cover always had an apt and often erudite aphorism or quote about reading: "I have gathered a posy of other men's flowers and nothing is mine but the cord that binds them" – Michel de Montaigne; "Everything in the world exists to end up in a book" – Stéphane Mallarmé. They have become collector's items.

Donald and Patricia Oresman had probably the world's largest collection of art organized around the theme of the reader; and they were generous in loaning works to museums. When Donald Oresman died in 2016, he left behind a unique monument to literature and to himself. Wordsworth's words could be his epitaph.

> Dreams, books are each a world: And books we know,
> Are a substantial world, both pure and good.
> Round these, with tendrils strong as flesh and blood
> Our pastime and our happiness will grow.

OPPOSITE Ingenious hidden storage is beautifully crafted, and no corner is unused. Unframed prints are kept in sliding shelves (left), while others, framed, are displayed on a series of openable panels (right) based on the secret hinged panels in Sir John Soane's Museum. ABOVE The fireplace, with its *trompe l'œil* painted marble surround, has Beckett's "Try again. Fail again. Fail better." inscribed on the hearth by letter-carver Simon Verity. On the wall of the gallery above is Donald Baechler's *Profile with Child Reading*. In the alcove to the left is a Picasso lithograph, *Jacqueline Lisant*.

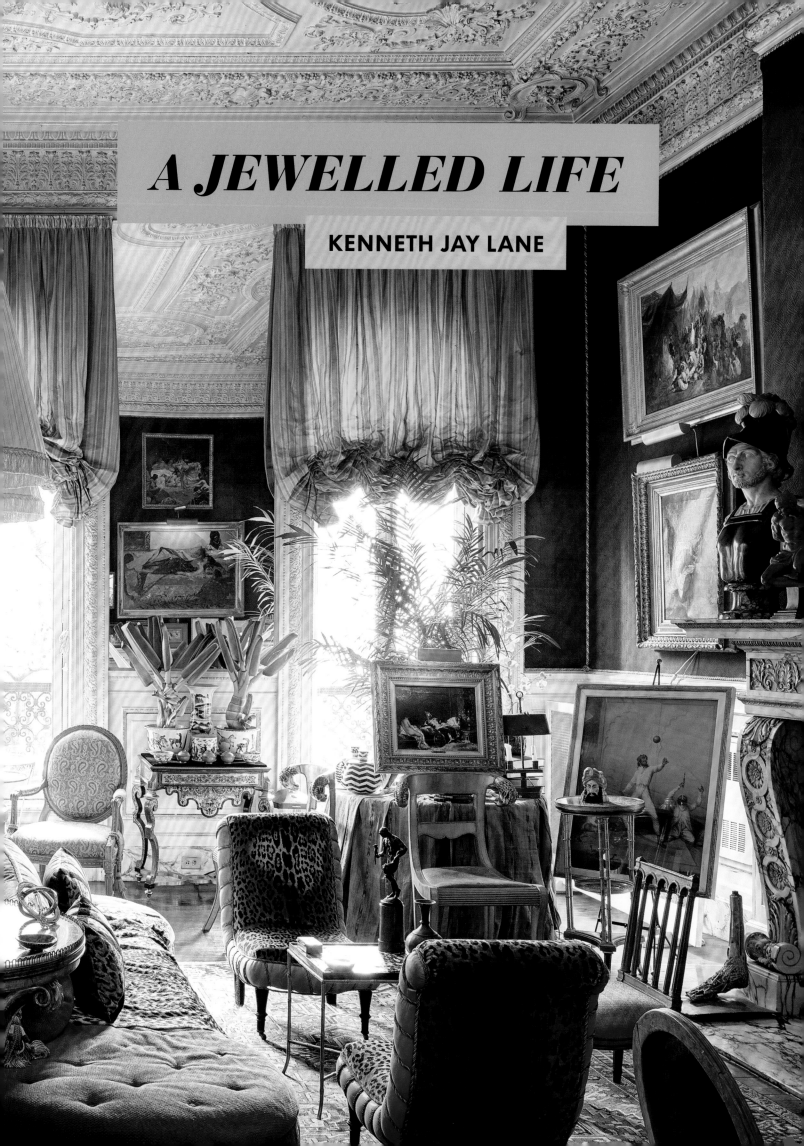

A JEWELLED LIFE

KENNETH JAY LANE

I'm in his apartment and it's glamorous. So is he. Beau Brummel. Witty. Irreverent. Handsome. Sly. And funny. A dandy. And sharp. Horribly so. Don't get off your guard. He still is all these things, though he is well into his eighties. And his apartment matches his character. He has a fine sardonic edge to his conversation and pretends not to take things seriously, but he didn't get to the top of his richly accoutred haute-boho tree through frivolity.

I first met him in the 1960s, when I was working at *Vogue* and he was *in* vogue, already one of the most iconic jewellery designers in the world. His fabulous ornaments channelled Schlumberger, Jeanne Toussaint, Fulco di Verdura, Bulgari, Cartier and Chanel - snakes and shells and puppy dogs' tails and whatever that singular eye of his happened upon was given its own rococo glittering spin. Every fashionable woman wanted this new fabulous "junque" jewellery.

He was once known as the King of Faux (even his book, an autobiography of his designs, is called *Faking It*), but now his jewellery is its own covetable thing. The Costume Institute of the Metropolitan Museum holds examples and some of his vintage pieces are collectors' items. He still works and loves it and sells any quantity of his new designs on television shopping channels to a new generation, all over the world. "I like to create jewellery that can be worn any time of the year, by any woman."

(Historical note - his jewellery has been worn by every First Lady since time began; Barbara Bush wore his three-strand pearl choker to her husband's Presidential Inaugural Ball and there's a famous photograph of Jacqueline Kennedy practically being strung up by John, her baby son, as he plays with her KJL triple-strand pearl necklace that she bought for less than two hundred dollars. It was sold at auction, after her death, for over two hundred thousand.)

He coins aphorisms at the drop of a cabochon. "Style and chic are not the same things. Chic is sort of being *au courant*. Style is not." "It's not what the woman has on her back, it's to do with her mind." 'Imagination is everything."

There is an element of the fabulous about both him and his *grande luxe* duplex in one of the handful of surviving mansions on Park Avenue, in the Murray neighborhood, built in the Italian Renaissance revival style by Stanford White of McKim, Mead & White. When it was finished in 1892 one of the founders of the Metropolitan Museum of Art, architectural critic Russell Sturgis, pronounced it "the most dignified structure in all the quarter of town, not a palace, but a fit dwelling house for a first-rate citizen." So Kenny, as his friends call him, has come home.

In the 1920s it was converted into the Advertising Club and in 1977 it was developed into apartments. Kenneth Jay, who lived in a swish little place nearby, watched progress with deep interest and an eagle eye, and before there was even a prospectus he gained access and wrote out a check for the only apartment with a balcony.

PAGES 36-37 In the sumptuous salon, orientalist paintings glow against the chocolatey Herculon-covered walls. French windows shaded by ruched tambour blinds overlook Park Avenue. OPPOSITE Two 17th-century marble busts of a male and a female warrior - regularly loaned to the Metropolitan Museum of Art - stand on the mantelpiece of the original Italian marble fireplace. The ceiling with its fine plasterwork is also original to the house; hanging from it are signature lamps from the venerable firm of Denning & Fourcade.

The balcony overlooks Park Avenue. "I love to stand there," he once said. "If I turn one way I can look all the way uptown. The other way and it's almost down to Union Square. If there's a snowstorm it's like being inside one of those glass paperweights which you shake so the snow falls." He was also seduced by the rare proportions of the place. "I think it's impossible to live in a room that isn't at least 13 feet high, he once said – without a blush – and here he found 16-foot-high ceilings and a chance to make another jewel of his own devising. He gutted most of what was there, keeping the vast original hand-carved Italian marble fireplace, but removing a marble staircase in the middle of what is now his distinctly opulent salon. He designed the interiors himself and his own master carpenter made the stairs and woodwork.

I love John Richardson's immortal words about the enormously rich eccentric *bon vivant* and nasty aesthete Charles de Beistegui: "A decorator of genius, Beistegui was fortunate in having a client of genius. Himself." Kenneth Lane is fortunate in being his own genius client – a master of rare objects and elusive space.

Once inside the double *trompe l'œil* walnut doors of his domain you're in the hall and dining room muffled with voluptuousness, a cantilevered staircase (which he designed himself) leading up past the scarlet red walls with their perfectly placed sconces up, up, up to a mezzanine balcony wherein is his library (and some enormous paintings and Chinese pots and garden stools) and thence to the hidden glories of his bedroom, patterned after the Paris apartment of Marie-Blanche de Polignac, the daughter of couturier Jeanne Lanvin. The mahogany and faux ebony surround of the overmantel and fireplace is copied from the Empire-inspired doors of her library, designed by architect Emilio Terry, and there are some wonderful paintings, including one of *The Sleep of Endymion* by Anne-Louis Girodet.

The main room, a 27-square-foot salon, wonderfully high, of course, with an elaborate molded plaster ceiling and a huge Heriz carpet, is a rich dialogue of color, harmony and contrast, visually and proportionally perfect, and inspires a sense of calm that is light years away from the tumult of Grand Central Station nearby.

The walls are hung with his collection of orientalist pictures, many by John Frederick Lewis, Jean-Léon Gérôme and Jean-Joseph Benjamin-Constant, and the mixture of textures and patterns, of different seating from sofas to ottomans to grand chairs (with a lot of faux leopard around), the elaborate ruffled curtains, the pictures and the polish give it the air of an American translation of English country house style – a little Edwardian – or grand Proustian French, with that twist of baroque fluency that is all his own. Urbane connoisseurship on show.

Tall faux palms flourish by the French windows, and the walls are close-hung with European as well as Pharaonic paintings (close-hanging is a skill that he has at his fingertips). The wall covering is chocolate-brown Herculon, a synthetic fiber mostly used for car upholstery but which under his alchemy looks deeply luxurious. The lighting of any great room is a giveaway of taste. He didn't want chandeliers so it's lit by huge arm lamps with fringed silk shades, the signature lamps of Robert Denning of Denning & Fourcade, a now defunct New York interior design firm known for extravagance and over-the-top opulence. They look clubby and terrific.

On every surface, including a Louis XIV Boulle Mazarin desk, and tables topped with *pietra dura*, pretty lamps and objects from all over are mixed and matched with insouciance. He places fanciful objects with amusement value ("silly things" he says, complacently, poking fun at himself – he's good at that) next to valuable rarities, "to take the curse off the good things!" Two mysterious-looking succulent plants like enormous cacti in Chinese blue and white planters turn out to be painted wooden bits of Indian mischief, and the cushions on a banquette are made from hand-woven dishcloths he found in the window of a shop selling kitchen stuff in Ahmedabad. These cohabit amiably with *objets de vertu* and proper treasures such as the discreetly placed little oval-topped North German ormolu and *alabastro fiorito* gueridon table (probably made in Berlin or Potsdam around 1800) with a pierced palmette cast border and frieze that he has promised to the Metropolitan Museum of Art. More treasures . . . the mantelshelf supports two ravishing Flemish late seventeenth-century busts of warriors, a male and a female, probably representing Mars and Minerva, in white and black stone marble on variegated red, black and grey and pink marble socles. They are quite at home here, surveying their territory, but each summer he lets them go off for a sojourn in the Met.

Although he says, with disconcerting honesty, "I'm a person who wants; I'm a wanter and a needer," he is a generous giver. His impressive collection of orientalist paintings and some of his furniture have been bequeathed to the Met, where there is a room named for him. "I have no children, so the world within my gallery will be my children."

Well, the world has always been his oyster. He was born in Detroit in 1932, "a Depression baby," visited Manhattan with his mother when he was fifteen and "fell madly in love with New York and that was that; I was never going back. I was an only child. I was a princeling." He smiles. "I have abdicated." He hasn't. He went everywhere, in every sense – he was an inveterate traveller as well as party-goer – knew everyone, hung out with the Duke and Duchess of Windsor in New York and France, was sketched by Andy Warhol in earlier days when he was designing shoes and Andy was drawing them, appeared in Warhol's films, and when in 1974 he married one of the beauties of her generation, an exquisite called Nicky Weymouth, he put the fashion feathers all a-flutter. (The rumor was that Beatrix Miller, the editor of British *Vogue*, had suggested the marriage, but in fact they met through Andy Warhol.) Nicky was the only Englishwoman I knew who wore Paris couture, and he has always been impeccably groomed. Together they were a destination style-sighting.

He has been collecting since he was a boy – "even as a teenager I used to covet and collect little ivory animals – worthless things but pretty, and coins and stamps and cigar bands – whatever

PAGE 40 Another seating area in front of a large bookcase with a carved pediment, one of a pair bought as double doors at auction. The pouffe is covered with tiger-skin fabric from Le Manach. PAGE 41 By the windows are a Louis XIV Boulle Mazarin desk, a pair of Louis XVI chairs covered in handwoven Indian fabric and an ormolu and *alabastro fiorito* gueridon with a pierced palmette cast edging. OPPOSITE In a corner of the salon, the cushions on the curved banquette are made from hand-woven dishcloths KJL found in Ahmedabad. The table was handmade for him in Agra. The second of the two matching pediments frames a door that leads to the dining room and his library and bedroom.

happened to those?" He holds out no hope for the addicts among us. "Once you buy two of the same thing you're a collector."

The first painting he bought and still loves is a portrait by Jean-Léon Gérôme of a Bashi-bazouk wearing a multicolored ikat and cone-shaped turban, with a fair few dangling tassels and gleaming weapons about his lovely person. Gérôme had an abiding fascination with these mad mercenaries of the Ottoman army who fought like the devil. I look them up: their name means "damaged head" or "crazy head," in the sense of uncontrollable and disorderly. No discipline whatsoever. "Yes, they were very naughty," he observes equably. He too seems to have a yearning for the exotic sensual world epitomized in Gérôme's paintings; and then too orientalism is a form of romanticism and KJL was a New Romantic before it was new.

Everything here has a provenance as well as a personal back story, sometimes capricious. The curious scarlet corded, leopard-covered chairs on each side of the fireplace he saw in a flea market in Palermo — "the chairs cost nothing so I had them brought back and covered them in the most expensive fabric you can imagine." The fabric was made by Maison Le Manach, a dream of a fabric house founded in France in 1829, which can

recreate any fabric — for a price. But the fabric on the chairs is nothing to the tiger-skin fabric, also from Le Manach, that covers the big pouffe at the other end of the room. This pouffe came from Pamela Harriman when she gave up her Fifth Avenue apartment. "It would cost $40,000 or $50,000 now to redo it," he muses. The needlepoint wing chair nearby, found in London at Christopher Gibbs, is the focus for another congenial seating area in front of a large ornamental bookcase with a carved pediment.

He has managed to make this huge room into an intimate, satisfying and charming place — the perfect backdrop for his parties. "I like to have people around," he says, in a bit of an understatement. "The dining room can seat eight or nine people but in here there can be forty. Sometimes it gets out of hand and there are almost seventy." His apartment is an affirmation of delight in the richness of things.

Oh! One last thing . . . a playing card — the seven of hearts — is stuck to a corner of the ceiling so high above. It's never fallen down and it has been there for years. "A magician just spun it up," he says, as if it were normal. "It was one of his tricks. Don't ask me how, darling, I'm not a magician." Oh, come on!

ABOVE LEFT A corner of KJL's bedroom. The overmantel and fireplace have a faux ebony surround modelled on the Empire-style doors of Comtesse Marie-Blanche de Polignac's library. ABOVE RIGHT KJL designed the staircase to the mezzanine.
OPPOSITE The plates on the dining table are copies of 19th-century Iznik pottery. The lamp is 19th-century American, and the sculpture behind is by the Danish artist Bertel Thorvaldsen. Two Chinese seats flank what KJL describes as "an unimportant cupboard." Not an adjective often used in this apartment.

ARTFULL

ROBERT LITTMAN & SULLY BONNELLY

Although Robert Littman and Sully Bonnelly's rectilinear and capacious apartment – perhaps better classified as a loft – is a stone's throw from the chaotic busyness of Union Square with its farmers' market, its chess games and musicians, once inside it's as tranquil and removed as a cloister. (Except for Lily, Ava and Vanya, the tumble of baleful tiny Brussels Griffons with their demonic eyes who seem to think that they are ten feet tall and built to match.)

But it's a cheerful cloister full of art and it flows in a wrap-around circle, rather like a slow-moving river punctuated along the way by art boulders, or the Stations of the Art, as it were, where you stop on the circuit to pay reverence to two Anselm Kiefers, a Sterling Ruby, Khmer stone sculptures, a big Sol LeWitt, pieces by Jenny Holzer, a Woodhenge by Carl Andre, a ramana drum from Thailand, a large Howard Hodgkin, an even larger David Hockney, and a wooden three-dimensional, bio-morphic leg splint by Charles and Ray Eames. A new result of the quest of the collector leans against the wall – a huge sensuous piece of hammered copper, part of a fragmentary replica of the Statue of Liberty by Danh Vo. ("I've been after it for while," Robert says, "and I finally got it in Paris.") Then you duck under Daisy Youngblood's plaster elephant's head protruding like a modern gargoyle, note a David Musgrave drawing – one of eight – propped casually against a bookshelf, glance at a John Cage drawing/score annotations and stop at a Shirazeh Houshiary. You salute a Scott Lyall painting and go back past the kitchen with its ceramics by Edmund de Waal, its John Baldessari, are tempted to sit on a Kuramata Lucite stool, fight off visual overkill and presto you're home again, soothed by the glorious Turneresque circle by Olafur Eliasson above two zigzag Gerrit Rietveld chairs. (Only don't dare to call it beautiful! – Eliasson didactically pronounced beauty a dangerous word, "because its been standardized into something kitsch.") Here you can collapse into a sofa beside a stainless steel and black laminate revolving coffee table designed with pizzazz by Willy Rizzo in 1969 and stare ahead at a piece by Richard Long or by Louise Bourgeois and – can that be a glass profile of Mussolini? In a black guest bathroom three Vija Celmins seduce the eye near to a Frank Lloyd Wright balustrade. "Where did you find that?" I inquire. "I've had it for ever," Robert says vaguely. "Maybe I bought it in Chicago."

There are not many places where a Carl Andre work and a Morandi etching flank a superb view of the Empire State Building. Here, art is a reality to be lived, and although the apartment carries a lot of zeitgeistic heft it is so edited that each work has its own reverberating space. The result is an open sesame of the imagination and an array of priorities and artistic instincts.

Robert swings for the fences when it comes to buying what he likes. "I wanted my museum – it's just in my blood," he says, "and so this is like curating a museum but in my house." And it's a living museum, since he is deeply prone both to changing things around and to acquiring new work all the time. Once, when I was visiting, two Andrée Putman chairs (channelled from Jean-Michel Frank's originals) arrived from the Wasserturm Hotel in Cologne to add to the three others she had earlier advised Robert to buy. Sully eyed them critically and allowed equally that he didn't like them. (Andrée Putman's pronouncement about loft living: "It is not about bathing in the living room and cooking in the bedroom but rather about opening spaces to various activities. Why should places be reduced to one function instead of favoring the sensations they bring us?" could well be Robert's creed.)

Besides the stand-out pieces there are other treasures strewn about – a bustier in plastic made by Issey Miyake for Grace Jones (they think) and another by Thierry Mugler are on points duty and two weather-worn carved wooden stands are intriguing. Robert says, "I was in a taxi in Kyoto passing an old shop and I saw something out of the corner of my eye, and I shouted stop – they were Kyoto temple pillars. Apparently they change the temple columns every ten years or so." They sit neatly under the Olafur Eliasson and beside the 1969 coffee table and near to two stone balls from the Taíno tribe, the indigenous people of the Dominican Republic who were decimated by Spanish colonists.

Robert was brought up in New York by parents who wanted him to be a lawyer ("I wasn't interested in school. I was interested in marching against Vietnam"), but who fed his artistic interests by taking him to concerts, shows and museums.

An influential friend of his father's, after a long talk to the young Robert, said to his father, "I'd let this man do what he wants to do." He has done just that ever since. He worked at the front desk of MoMA and at the Kornblee Gallery while at postgraduate studies at NYU's Institute of Fine Arts, where Noma Copley and Daisy (Margaret – married to Alfred H. Barr, the director of MoMA) were his classmates on a Friday evening seminar on the Bronze Age in the Aegean. He sat between them and would nudge them awake when they dozed off.

A life-changing moment arrived when Noma Copley invited him to her apartment. She had been married to the painter William Copley, who in the 1950s had opened an art gallery in Beverly Hills where he showed works by René Magritte, Max Ernst, Yves Tanguy, Roberto Matta, Joseph Cornell and Man Ray. It was not a success there – too far in advance of the dozy film town – and he bought the stuff that did not sell. (His collection was sold at auction in 1979 for $6.7 million, at the time the highest total for a single owner's collection in the United States.) Robert remembers the shock of his visit: "When she opened the door it was one of the most amazing things I have ever seen in my life. There were at least three Balthuses, Man Ray's *Lips*, Duchamp's *Chess Table* – it was just full of astonishing things." I felt a bit like that when the elevator door opened to Robert's apartment and I stepped under the glare stare of the marble surveillance camera by Ai Weiwei into a disarranged

PAGES 46-7 Lily, Ava and Vanya survey the art from their bedroom vantage point. On the floor, a crumpled sheet metal sculpture by John Chamberlain in front of a wooden piece by Carl Andre and, leaping out from the wall, a simian figure by Daisy Youngblood. On the opposite wall is an abstract by Cheyney Thompson and on the shelf above the bed one of Charles and Ray Eames's iconic – and practical – leg splints; on the shelf below is a David Hockney iPad drawing. OPPOSITE, CLOCKWISE FROM TOP A marble Jenny Holzer bench sits near the iconic egg chair by Arne Jacobsen; a Rachel Whiteread floor piece rests near a John Chamberlain sculpture with, behind, the geometric forms of a Donald Judd piece on the wall; a large Sterling Ruby collage sits on the chest of drawers next to a Roman urn. A small Rachel Whiteread sculpture above Khmer stone figures and a Giorgio Morandi still life. Above a black marble shelf are two Jenny Holzer pieces – one a plaque, the other a condom – bearing the same message.

Carl Andre piece, a splendid resin cast of a London door by Rachel Whiteread and the demonic-looking Griffons in a tumble of rage.

His life underwent another upheaval in 1983 when, as director of the Grey Art Gallery NYU, he was in Mexico City researching Frida Kahlo loans for a prospective show. He suggested to a friend, Alberto Raurell, the new young director of the Tamayo Museum (which under his guidance was rapidly becoming a center of international painting, jazz and theater) that the exhibition "Hockney Paints the Stage," a now famous collaboration between Hockney and Martin Friedman, director of the Walker Art Center in Minneapolis, would be a good show for the Tamayo. Robert made the introductions and, as he recalls, "arrangements proceeded apace." Tragedy followed. He was in Paris organizing a Jean Cocteau exhibition for the Grey Gallery (which, as it turned out, was to be his final show there) when he got the telephone call with the news that Alberto Raurell had been murdered in a restaurant hold-up. He was asked if he could come to Mexico and

help to finish installing the Hockney show. "I went down and never left." He was for many years the curator of the Jacques and Natasha Gelman Collection and is now president of the Vergel Foundation, a collection of modern and contemporary Mexican art (including many famous Frida Kahlo paintings) which is based in New York and Cuernavaca and is shown in museums around the world.

The first time Sully and Robert went out together on a date, thirty-three years ago (they married in 2012, soon after it became legally possible), they went to one art show, then many art shows and later the same day Robert bought a chair. Not any old chair. So Sully learned fast what Robert's life-focus was, and now, Sully says, "We buy together and consult each other." Sully was born in Santo Domingo, graduated from the Parsons School of Design and worked for fashion houses including Oscar de la Renta, Bill Blass and Isaac Mizrahi. He is now the creative director of his own eponymous business.

They travel all over to look at art, in galleries, exhibitions and museums as well as attending the openings of the Vergel

ABOVE In the living room a serene circular piece by Olafur Eliasson looks out over two Gerrit Rietveld chairs, the crumpled metal of a John Chamberlain sculpture and a stainless steel and black laminate coffee table by Willy Rizzo. A Daisy Youngblood elephant head juts out from the wall.

Foundation exhibitions. I ask about the dual watercolor portrait of them together, painted by David Hockney in 2002. Where is it? "In storage," Robert admits, "– tired of looking at ourselves like Gertrude Stein and Alice B. Toklas!"

Sully's collection is on the other side of that entrance foyer in a set of quiet rooms with an Agnes Martin that pulls at the heartstrings, day beds by Mies van der Rohe, a Fornasetti table and a Plexiglas box sculpture by Robert Graham; here on white shelves are myriad white pottery vases – used by flower shops from the 1930s right up to the 1950s for sending flowers. Their various shapes and cream and white finishes suggest both the vases made by Constance Spry in London and those found in Jean-Michel Frank's eclectic Paris shop. Basically these are the takeaway disposable containers of the time and the taste of the period comes shining through; now they are much sought-after objects. Sully buys them wherever he sees them. (When he bought the Fornasetti table it was in the happy belief that it was patterned with drawings of croissants. Robert had gently to point out that they were penises and perhaps it would be

judicious to choose another pattern. He opted for some architectural designs.)

Robert came by this loft in a sideways sort of way – a posh apartment on the Upper East Side was to be provided as part of his signing agreement on leaving Manhattan to go to Mexico. Didn't want to live uptown. Not his style. "When I saw this huge, bare loft, part of the Photo Arts Building and in a fearful state – the floor painted black, the windows blacked out and full of photographic equipment – I said, 'This is where I want to live.' Union Square was the stationery district of New York at that time, and it was very run-down. Didn't matter."

When Picasso installed himself in a new place, he did drawings of the area to map out a kind of cosmology. This is what Robert did. Then an architect helped to make practical sense of his plans for knocking down walls (and he and Sully fought about it all). It took eight months of construction work, freeing up the space, to make what is in effect a gallery within a comfortable home. The result over thirty years later is an open sesame of the imagination, full of peace, appalling barking, and did I mention Art?

ABOVE In a passage, David Hockney's *The Arrival of Spring*, an iPad drawing printed on four sheets of paper, overlooks a Carl Andre floor piece and two Khmer stone figures ext to a copper fragment by Danh Vo. PAGES 52–53 In the office, an Agnes Martin painting and a collection of white pottery flower vases provide a cool backdrop to a Piero Fornasetti table, a Jean Prouvé stool, Verner Panton's iconic chair and (at left) a Larry Bell cube and (right) a Plexiglas box sculpture by Robert Graham.

ABOVE Also in the office, a painting of a gorilla, *Kong*, by Walton Ford, below a clay figure by Rebecca Warren. On the wall, a twisting sculpture by John Chamberlain and in the center a piece by Sterling Ruby and a suspended ribbon form by Miroslaw Balka. On a shelf behind sits a green bustier by Issey Miyake.

ABOVE Works in the raised corner space include a circular piece by Richard Long, a Khmer stone figure and a clear glass Mussolini vase by Karim Rashid. In the foreground, a bronze head by Martin Puryear overlooks a pink glass sculpture by Roni Horn.

FELICITATIONS

PAYNE WHITNEY

It's not often you walk into a house and have your breath taken away by a marvel of a room. This happened to me in the old Payne Whitney mansion, a unique retreat on Fifth Avenue in a handsome Beaux Arts building garlanded with ivy, in the middle of Museum Mile, just down across the street from the Metropolitan Museum of Art. And, oh, joy! It has the ultimate luxury of a garden oasis with shady trees and a birch grove. (Called the Florence Gould Garden, its new design in 2000 was made possible by the eponymous Foundation.) In fact, since the entire block in which the house stands remains much as it was when built to ordained residential scale in the early twentieth century, one has a vision of a vanished grand old Fifth Avenue before most of it was developed into high rise apartments.

The building has been owned by the French government since 1952, when Claude Lévi-Strauss, the father of modern anthropology and the first French cultural counsellor to the United States, cleverly persuaded his government to buy it. It now houses the Cultural Services department of the French embassy,

The Payne Whitney house is both an important relic of New York's Gilded Age and a heartening example of how an atavistic mansion can be turned into a modern thriving sanctuary of culture, learning and enjoyment. (Incidentally, the term the Gilded Age was first used by Mark Twain, derogatively – as gilded refers to a veneer on a baser substance, "hardened into a brazen gaudiness." Not applicable here, fortunately.) It was built in the first decade of the twentieth century by the architectural company McKim, Mead & White and, though identified as the work of the collective firm, it was actually designed by Stanford White, whose design principles embodied the self-confident American renaissance of the time. American wealth was amassed in a flash and they built their houses in a flash, using European models to make a show of opulence signifying the existence of an aristocratic caste in a democratic city.

The house was a wedding present to a rich and prominent New Yorker, Payne Whitney, from his uncle, Colonel Oliver Payne. The Colonel had bought the plot of land in 1902 for $625,000 (over $15,000,000 in today's figures) and spent at least as much again building the house. Payne's bride, Helen Hay, was a writer, successful racehorse breeder, patron of the arts and poet – known as the Poetess of the Ballroom. (Her father had confiscated nearly all copies of her first book of poetry for fear of embarrassing the family.) She lived in the house in great style until her death in 1944.

It is one of Stanford White's most successful monuments, granite, bow-fronted, with fine carved details and entablatures between its five stories. He oversaw every detail and spent more than $350,000 in Europe for the young couple, buying statues, paintings, tapestries, furniture, rugs and lamps, as well as mantels, columns, stained glass, wood panelling and a gilded oak portico.

He had finalized the aesthetic details and was still supervising the construction of the exterior and interiors when, in June 1906,

The Rotunda, viewed from east to west with the entrance doors framing a replica of Michelangelo's young archer.

57

he was shot dead by a jealous husband in a scandalous affair which reverberated in New York for decades. (A film, *The Girl in the Red Velvet Swing*, was made about the murder.)

It isn't obvious from the street that part of this building is open to the public. For tucked into the mansion is the best, the only French bookshop in New York. (The last one, the Librairie de France, closed in 2009.)

So. Venturing into a spectacular rotunda through the carved pilastered entrance with its wrought-iron doors is to be taken out of New York life's jazzy rhythm (never ordinary at the best of times) and into another kind of Gallic harmony. The shallow-domed circular hall, for all its gleaming marble, is slightly crepuscular. A ring of eight pairs of veined marble pillars supports a domed ceiling decorated with lattice and vines. In the center a rebarbative iron rail protects a marble fountain designed by Stanford White; and on the fountain stands (in a manner of speaking, since his legs are somewhat truncated) a marble statue of a young archer. This is a replica, as the original, which White bought in Rome, is now thought – amid much fevered excitement – to be an early work by Michelangelo, and is on loan to the Metropolitan Museum. This replica was produced by computerized 3D modelling

The painted ceiling has a curious anaglyptic look with roundels of vapid scenes of children and dogs and bas-reliefs of cherubs at play; there is still the rose in the center from which a chandelier once hung.

And now to the bookshop. This little delight – called Albertine Books, in homage to Proust – has more than fourteen thousand contemporary and classic titles in French and English, from thirty French-speaking countries. It opened in September 2014 and it owes its existence to the imagination and daring of the then cultural counsellor for the embassy, Antonin Baudry (now editor of the *Paris Review*). He lamented the loss of a French bookshop and meeting place in the city and set about looking for ways to launch a new one. In a *coup de foudre* he realized he could make one inside the Cultural Services building – no rent! – and at the same time fulfill his desire to let New Yorkers see how beautiful the interior was. "It made no sense that such an international city didn't have a French bookstore," Baudry said in a interview. "Francophone New Yorkers were coming back from Paris with suitcases crammed with books. And this building is part of the patrimony of New York. Now the doors are open."

The architect Jacques Garcia did a fabulous conversion of some old offices. Through the doors up the stairs (not the grandiose marble stairs which featured in *Gone with the Wind*), past the huge windows, is a browserie where you can sit on a sofa or pretty chairs and read to your heart's content under the huge hanging amber-shaded lights by Garcia, like art installations in themselves. "I want this to be a place that has a soul," Baudry said, and he got his wish. You could be in a corner of the Palais Mazarin. The celadon-painted bookcases, outlined with burnished trim and sconces with miniature shades matching those of the hanging lamps, carry a row of busts from the Louvre atelier, of writers and savants from Descartes to Camus. Plus Benjamin Franklin. Voltaire of course is looking down. It wouldn't be properly French if he weren't.

Jacques Garcia once said, "I am, before everything, a creator of atmosphere," and he has certainly followed his precept through here. Its astrological blue and gold ceiling was painted by artisans in France after the starry sky painting created by the symbolist painter Franz von Stuck in the music room of his villa in Munich. Talk about *luxe, calme et volupté*.

But the room that makes you hold your breath is on the first floor. It is one of the most stunning rooms in all of America: this exquisite, over-the-top, extravagant, pellucid, precious little mirrored jewel box is called, not without reason, the Venetian Room. Mirrored walls with gilded composition fittings, a gold-leafed metal latticework cove with vining porcelain flowers, antique French and Italian portraits in gilt frames with putti, oak wainscoting, a herringbone parquet floor and neoclassical ornaments surrounding the large mirrored panels make for a grotto Narcissus might have died for. (Still, the huge elaborately carved marble fireplace, quite out of place, might have brought him back to his senses.)

White had approved the final details shortly before his death in 1906 and his final drawings show the room almost exactly as it appears today. Helen Hay Whitney loved the room and although after her death the house and furniture were sold, her son, Jock Whitney, followed her wish that the room be preserved. It was dismantled and remained in storage in the stables at their country estate in seventy-five hermetically sealed wooden packing cases until 1997, when Jock's widow, Betsey Cushing Whitney, donated the room to the French-American Foundation and provided the financial support for its restoration.

It's a room from a mini palazzo; you feel the waters of a Venetian canal must be rippling outside. Yet for all the outpouring of luxury and conspicuous consumption, there is an air about this room that avoids pretension and gives it a forlorn beauty.

Voltaire wrote: "Appreciation is a wonderful thing: It makes what is excellent in others belong to us as well." What's so wonderful is that this excellence belongs to anyone who walks through these doors.

PAGES 58–59 The Venetian Room, just off the Rotunda. OPPOSITE The Marble Room doorway, leading into the second floor of Albertine Bookstore.

ARCANIA

GORDON VENEKLASEN

Gordon VeneKlasen loves his house and it shows; its interior is a demonstration of how to make peaceful sense of the dizzy international art world in which he lives. It reflects the personality of the owner and what lies behind is the aesthetic history of his life and his endless curiosity.

He is the managing partner and co-owner of the Michael Werner Gallery in New York and London, a heavy hitter in the art world, and is always on the go - in every sense - curious, febrile, restless, flying all over the world, dealing with the relentless churn of art dealing now.

It's quiet in this house in the heart of Greenwich Village, save for birdsong coming through open windows. How can this be, in chaotic downtown New York? We are in MacDougal Alley, one of the last ten mews left in Manhattan, built in 1833 and called after Alexander McDougall, a Revolutionary War military leader. The little enclave lies behind cast-iron gates, with one small entrance usually open so you can wander through to your heart's delight, envying the lucky people who live here. And lived. They are many and distinguished - including Jackson Pollock, Noguchi and Jeff Koons.

Gordon VeneKlasen knew the house and on hearing that the owners were moving asked them what they planned to do with it. "Sell it; do you want to buy it?" He bought it. Full stop. It didn't go to market. That's what he's like. Snap.

He had been living happily enough in an enviable location – Gramercy Park. "I loved it. It was too small, stuff stacked up – but I loved it. Yet when I left, though thinking I would be so sad, I closed the door with relief. I am so happy to be here and I love the silence."

The house, 1,920 square feet over three floors, seems much larger, with its cutaway ceilings giving a high airy feeling, its different levels, its ranging staircases. These are part of an earlier conversion, but his great friend the architect Annabelle Selldorf made radical changes with her usual elegant and intelligent approach, turning a bedroom into the kitchen, a wine cellar into a library and creating a new top-floor terrace. She also designed the terrace's faded teak table and the fountain with its plangent sounds of water, as well as some of the furniture in the house. She knows Gordon so well that she delivered the house he craved without much discussion.

He has made a narrative of his life here, in every room, in the felicitous arrangements of the works, avant-garde, nuanced and rare, he has collected. Indeed, there is almost an air of meditation, a light liturgical quality in the atmosphere. Annabelle Selldorf once described him as "the most curious and voracious person I've ever met; he wants it all."

Coming in from the mews, one is enclosed in her solution to the knotty problem of entering a living area directly from the street. A glass box creates a viewpoint from which to take stock of the designated spaces ahead - dining room, sitting room, kitchen, stretching the width and length of the house, with a staircase rising to one side. It's an eye-popping eyeful and a lesson in punctuation arrangement; but this is not a house to be taken in with an easy prospecting glance.

Gallery director, art dealer, and original and sensitive curator, VeneKlasen has boundless energy and an eye like a bandit for a hidden treasure. He joined the Michael Werner Gallery in 1990. It was founded, as Galerie Werner, in 1963 in Berlin by Michael Werner, somewhat of a legend in the art world, who now lives in Germany. He first showed the work of unknown German artists, including Georg Baselitz, Sigmar Polke, A. R. Penck, Jörg Immendorff, all young and incandescent, who changed the face of art in the sixties and seventies and are now giant stars of the art world. They came of age with Werner; and VeneKlasen has this same drive to find and nourish young rising stars. He understands the creative impulse, is a passionate supporter of his artists, who include Peter Doig, Enrico David and Kai Althoff, and owns many of their works. You'll also come across pieces by R. Crumb, Bruce Conner and many others out there kicking at the edges, and even one by the Franco-Russian artist Serge Charchoune, who tried his hand at so many styles that he slips between the interstices of definition. Salvador Dalí is there too. Gordon has always admired the work of the now-fashionable painter Francis Picabia, and his collection includes a drawing of Meraud Guinness – the Irish painter, writer and poet who was Picabia's protégée, his model and his mistress – as well as a fine painting of a nude, which hangs on a staircase wall.

On the same staircase there is a painting called Strange Adventure – a gift from his friend, the generous, daring artist Sigmar Polke, who created some of the most ravishing paintings and photographs of the last forty years. Polke photographed this painting in everyday places – say, a parking lot – and later gave Gordon the painting accompanied by the photographs, as a birthday present. These photographs aren't on display but, but on another birthday he and Polke were in a studio looking over photographs for, as Gordon thought, an exhibition. "And then he turned to me and said, 'Happy Birthday,' and gave them to me." These now hang in his living room.

The living room is on the second floor, where, at one end, silken light spills through 10-foot-high windows with pink and gold curtains in a Fortuny fabric. This light-filled, beguiling room is full of treasures. You could learn a great deal about various recherché epochs of art just by asking questions in this house. That elaborate gilded cartwheel hanging from the ceiling? It's a nineteenth-century giltwood and zinc chandelier from Glienicke Palace, designed by Karl Friedrich Schinkel for Prince Carl of Prussia in 1826; and it replaced a James Turrell light installation. "A ridiculous thing to have in a private house," VeneKlasen says.

The walls of the powder room are made from old leached-copper roofing found in a Brooklyn building yard. The copper shimmers with different colors and different lights.

Michael Werner first introduced him to Schinkel's work and then Gordon saw more of it in the V&A and became hooked. This is something which, it is apparent, happens to him quite a lot. He does love the arcane and is fascinated by reliquaries and mystical objects and their innate power. Curious long thingies made of carved ivory are nestling modestly on the bottom shelf of a table. "What are those?" I ask. VeneKlasen had the same reaction when he saw one for the first time, in a store on the Upper East Side, twenty-five years ago. "I said, 'What is that?' It reminded me of the Duchamp *Stoppages*. It looked so contemporary and I fell for it and started collecting them." Well, they're *hu* court tablets, memoranda and ritual implements from the Ming dynasty required for formal dress and used as symbols of rank for gaining access to the emperor. Officials shielded their mouths with their *hu* when speaking to the god-like figure on the imperial throne. They are not easy to come by, but he has a fine collection now.

Above the fireplace hangs a triangle-shaped multi-panel drawing from Kai Althoff and nearby is the magnificent painting *Pelican Island* by Peter Doig. On the hearth lies a carved flint like a tapered club that could do you a lot of mischief. A fertility object from the Yemen. Rare. Of course. More diverse objects of curious provenance – a German seventeenth-century carved wood skull here, a checkerboard by Italian sculptor

Enrico David there. A nineteenth-century Tibetan ritual vessel sits atop a grand table. Very grand. Designed by Robert Adam, it's from Apsley House, the London home of the Duke of Wellington. The Duke replaced the stone top with granite he brought back from his campaign against Napoleon in Egypt. "I bought it from a dealer who lent me the table for an Adam house in Mansfield Street we rented as our first gallery in London," Gordon says. "When we left, the table came with me." (He left to open a new gallery in Upper Brook Street in Mayfair.) The writing desk table at the other end of the room is by the royal cabinetmaker Johannes Klinkerfuss, and belonged to one of the kings of Württemberg. In a historically piquant juxtaposition a painting by A.R. Penck, painter, printmaker, sculptor and zealot jazz drummer, born in East Germany, hangs near it. Penck's real name is Ralf Winkler, and he, along with a group of other Neo-Expressionist painters, was considered dangerously subversive by the GDR regime. By the late 1960s, Penck's work was largely banned from public view, which, as VeneKlasen says, "made him unable to show his work for a very long time." Artists like Georg Baselitz and supporters like Michael Werner helped to smuggle his work out of East Germany and Penck garnered recognition in the international art world.

On the other side of the room is Gordon's exquisite collection of twentieth-century Venetian master glassblowers' vases; he only

OPPOSITE A nude by Francis Picabia (1942) hangs beside the staircase. ABOVE The focal point of the living room is Karl Friedrich Schinkel's giltwood and zinc chandelier. Over the fireplace is a multi-panel drawing by Kai Althoff, which recently formed part of an exhibition at MoMA.

had to see one, a black and red piece by Napoleone Martinuzzi, to be out like a truffle hound in Venice to unearth more. Most of the glass is by Martinuzzi but he also has pieces by the revered Italian architect Carlos Scarpa, who, having learned the art of glassblowing at the Venini glassworks in Murano, redefined its possibilities and parameters.

It all combines with domestic touches such as a rosy velvet sofa designed by Annabelle Selldorf in the colors of a favorite cashmere scarf, to make a rich art vein of a room.

There are, of course, paintings everywhere. Some might seem surprisingly out of context, but they reveal the breadth of VeneKlasen's passions and interests. On the first floor a Puvis de Chavannes hangs near a Cornelius Polenberg, a piece by Carl Andre and a seventeenth-century study for a painting of Lazarus; a little watercolor by Victor Hugo is next to one by Karl Hubbuch, and a drawing by Andy Warhol (one of many) is in dialogue with a work by James Lee Byars. Propped on a chair is a painting by David Harrison, whose work often explores a world where natural and supernatural go hand in hand — a realm not far from VeneKlasen's imagination. Above the fireplace hangs a painting, *Salamander Stone*, by Sigmar Polke, whose death Gordon still mourns. A pair of Paolo Buffa slipper chairs faces down the chaise longue by Edward Wormley — a coveted American designer of early modernist furniture — which is covered with such panache in old Turkish fabric that it looks almost Byzantine. A glass table by Gio Ponti (with a yellow Arp-like Italian lamp about to take off beside it) keeps the peace between them.

On the other side of the room a polished bookcase full of fine things is made of Brazilian ebonized wood, and the dining table and chairs are by the pioneer of modernist Brazilian furniture, architect Joaquim Tenreiro. "I got it in my head to collect Brazilian furniture, and when I was in Rio I went to dinner and I saw a chair by Joaquim Tenreiro. The next day I asked where they had got it and by the end of the day I was ahead! I went all over and purchased a bunch."

It's a lovely room and, like his library, in the basement, with its vast collection of books and also replete with remarkable things, it is conducive to rest and talk.

In his bedroom with its high windows he awakens to a sixteenth-century Italian shiver-making etching — *Regalia of the Dead* — a memento mori, hung at eye level. But, countering its gloom, a vivid still life of three apples by Courbet and a collection of Warhol shadow paintings are hung nearby. More gloom with a none-too-subtle Ed Ruscha drawing, called *Three Darvon, Three Seconal*, of opiate pills falling through a fog.

His powder room is something to behold. He and Anabelle Selldorf installed walls made from century-old leached-copper roofing found in a Brooklyn building yard. The copper shimmers with different colors and different lights. It's hallucinatory. VeneKlasen once compared the effect to the Warhol oxidation piss paintings produced by using urine on canvases coated with copper metallic paint.

Where did this paragon of taste and rigorous line (and successful dealing, as everyone is quick to tell me) come from? He grew up in Santa Fe where his father was a geologist. He studied

A large part of VeneKlasen's collection of glass is displayed on shelves and a table in the living room. The table and chairs by Joaquim Tenreiro pin down a 19th-century Moroccan carpet.

art history, did a term at the Ashmolean in Oxford, then went to Spain on a year-long study abroad program and spent a lot of time at the Prado. "I dreamed of being cosmopolitan and Madrid was the epitome of that dream." In the late eighties he spent a year in Zimbabwe with his sister, Lisa, who was working on women's rights efforts. "When I came back to New York I was exhausted and thought I didn't want to be involved with the art business." But once Michael Werner came calling he became committed.

"What makes a collector?" that doyen of antique dealers Christopher Gibbs once asked – and answered, "Damage and at the art of looking. Really looking." VeneKlasen really looks. Then too there is that secret magnetic force that every collector experiences, which somehow attracts the things desired to the one who covets. Basically things provide magic protection; they shield the collector. There is quite a lot of magic one way or another in this house.

OPPOSITE The dining table and chairs are by Joaquim Tenreiro. On top of the polished ebonized wood bookcase, and surrounded by notable artworks, are two handsome candlesticks. VeneKlasen found these in India. Costing the equivalent of 50 cents, they were more expensive to bring back than to buy. ABOVE A subtle glass and wood structure encloses the entrance area, protecting the house from the elements without detracting from the openness. Sigmar Polke's *Salamander Stone* (1998) hangs above the fireplace.

INTELLECTUAL EDEN

GINI ALHADEFF & FRANCESCO PELLIZZI

MEMPHIS IN CHELSEA

ARMAND LIMNANDER

Armand Limnander, the chic executive editor of *W* magazine, doesn't behave like a certified obsessive — but the evidence is revealed in his captivating, witty apartment in the heart of Chelsea, a shrine to a style he has pursued with a scouting and shriving eye for years — ferreting out the best examples of the objects and furniture made by the Italian design collective known as the Memphis Group.

This postmodernist amalgamation of designers, the enfants terribles of 1980s design, led by Ettore Sottsass, began in the apartment of Sottsass's wife, Barbara Radice, in Milan in December 1980. The odd name comes from the fact — or legend — that while the group were incubating their then-revolutionary ideas they listened to the Bob Dylan song "Stuck inside of Mobile with the Memphis Blues Again" on a loop.

Sottsass, in his sixties and already a famed Italian designer, had invited a group of young designers to develop a new furniture collection to show at the next Milan Furniture Fair. They tossed into the air given ideas about what "normal" furniture looked like, and contrived the mix of exuberance, glittery kitsch and sheer genius which was unveiled at the show to general bemusement. It was a zoom into futuristic space and was labelled anarchic, crazy and subversive; but what was launched there has continued to influence not just furniture design but art and graphics. Barbara Radice said: "You should not imagine that we would sit around and actually talk about 'the future of design.' There was a necessity of updating figurative language because what was around, as Ettore used to say, after a while felt like chewing cardboard." The "less is more" design of the prevalent concepts of modernism and minimalism was kicked into touch and what has been described as "the fusion of avant-garde with rock'n'roll kitsch" took center stage. Plastics, Formica, laminations, lacquered and painted wood, colored glass, dizzy colors — turquoise, yellow, scarlet, ultramarine —were part and parcel of the design reference, as was asymmetry, surprise and general skylarking. The Memphis style channelled American 1950s design — diners and soda fountains, pink flashy-tailed Cadillacs — hectic advertising, laminates, plastics. Many beholders recoiled at the brash in-your-faceness of the pieces; others fell on the objects with avidity — witness Armand on the prowl thirty-five years later, one of many young collectors now. "It looked like a prank," David Bowie, who was also a collector, once wrote. "It sucked on the breath of pop culture with gusto and an enthusiasm that was delightful to witness."

When a friend who has an apartment as far removed in design and concept as is possible from this one suggested I see this cabinet of esoteric curiosities I hastened over to Chelsea. "I love the statement that is Armand's apartment," he said. "He has a whole homage to that hideous eighties Memphis group — it's an amazing set piece."

You can say that again. Deep breath. Armand has not just evoked but has resurrected the colorful mad swagger of the conceit and has held it down firmly with his stern exactitude.

(Not that he doesn't also introduce slapstick humor — as, for instance, in two beefburger beanbags from Urban Outfitters.)

Then again, this little temple tucked away on prosaic West 20th street is not fanatically Memphis, as at first it might appear — iconic original pieces are mixed with decidedly contemporary furniture and art with the same playful spirit of irreverence as Memphis. Yet it's also practical, a real design for living. *Tutti* comforts. It's in a building dating from 1936. "There are so many cookie-cutter apartments in New York — and I wanted character," he says. "I didn't want to live in a box cut up from a commercial building. And there are windows everywhere, which is very important to me."

He is modest about its remarkability and assured me before I visited it that scouting it would be "a task that I'm sure can be accomplished in mere seconds." Not so. It's an education in mannerism and aesthetic accomplishment — not an evocation of a culture but a homage to it. And an excursion into Armand's quest to winkle out rarities. He constantly changes things around and banishes others. "I have strong tastes and I edit what I like. I don't have storage and if it doesn't sit well, out it goes."

It is impeccably arranged and edited so that the very air seems limned as if one is inside the making of a work of art using Emily Dickinson grey and then exploding Walt Whitman colors within. And it's so soigné. There's not one unconsidered line in this design capsule — the fruit in the sawtoothed bowl by Masanori Umeda (if you can call such an object a bowl) looks as though it has been grown to highlight the saucy poise of the blue dining table by Michele de Lucchi.

What pulls it together so miraculously is the compositional tension of the lovely tenebrous grey color stealing over the walls, the doors, the ceilings, the radiators, uniting the whole space and place and making it seem larger than it is.

The floor is a kaleidoscope of color: he found the dazzling carpet — "Angle de la Lumière," designed by the painter and sculptor Guy de Rougemont — at Phillips auction house; and his bed, by the Seattle-based artist, designer, architect and furniture-maker Roy McMakin, he found in Chicago, at Wright auctions, which specializes in rare twentieth-century pieces. He covered it in a fabric designed by Ettore Sottsass — and the chairs around the dining table are all a standard Sottsass design made before Memphis was a twinkle in his eye. Armand covered them in vintage fabric from George Sowden and Nathalie du Pasquier, and very fine they look.

"I'd love to be a serious collector," he says. "But I'm not a collector in the real sense — if I were I would collect art." He does in fact collect paintings pretty thoroughly. Above one of two identical sofas by Richard Woods and Sebastian Wrong is a big piece by Wyatt Kahn, whose work often crosses the line from painting into sculpture: he cuts unprimed canvases into shapes and pieces them together. On other walls are works by Nick van Woert, Matt Connors, the Canadian artist Paul P., and an intricate sand painting by Californian Jennifer Guidi.

PAGES 78–79 In the dining area Armand has recovered the Ettore Sottsass chairs in vintage fabric by Memphis designers Nathalie du Pasquier and George Sowden. The table is by Michele de Lucchi, and the sawtoothed fruit bowl is "Parana," a ceramic piece created for Memphis by Masanori Umeda. OPPOSITE One of the rarest pieces in Armand's collection is Michele de Lucchi's "Phoenix" bookcase. Next to it a pedestal by Ettore Sottsass supports Alex Israel's *Maltese Falcon* sculpture. Above is a painting by Canadian artist Paul P. PAGES 82–83 Leaping out of the living room, the bright colors of the carpet by Guy de Rougemont and the ceiling light by Vico Magistretti are matched by Memphis's floor lamps (Sottsass), yellow side table (de Lucchi) and blind fabric by Nathalie du Pasquier. Above matching sofas by Richard Woods and Sebastian Wrong are artworks by Wyatt Kahn (left) and Nick van Woert (right). The provocative vase is by Sottsass, and the gnomes are flea-market finds.

All the paintings answer to the demands made by an environment that could well be overwhelming. Instead there is a dialogue partly instigated by the clever hang of each piece. It becomes a narrative about someone extraordinary, hidden, but whose taste lives here out in the open.

Armand Limnander is half French, half Columbian, grew up in Bogotá and from an early age learned how to look – his family always loved to travel, to see, to explore and discover things. He studied at Berkeley and Columbia and moved to New York in 1996 to work in fashion journalism, including stints at *Vogue* and as features director of *T: The New York Times Style Magazine*, where he had a formative experience. "I was the last person to interview Sottsass. He died two months after the interview. We were working on our design issue and I heard he was ill. I asked his wife, Barbara Radice, if I could interview him. She said, 'He's at home, he gets tired very easily but he could do a short interview.' We had a feature on the last page where we asked someone to choose something which meant a lot to him or her. I asked him about the thing he would choose and he knew instantly. A series of vases. He had gone to India in the 1960s and had become very ill. He nearly died. When he returned to Italy and recovered he made these vases – his all-time favorites."

One of the most extraordinary pieces in the apartment is the big glamorous bookcase – the "Phoenix" by Michele de Lucchi. "It's very special. It's an early piece by the group – there are only two in existence – and that's very de Lucchi, that cladding over plastic. I found it on eBay." I look startled. "Yes! The guy who sold it was a blue-collar worker and I asked him why do you have this? It turned out that in the nineties he worked for Artemide, the Memphis showroom in New York. When it was closing down the president of the company told him he could choose one piece – and he chose this bookcase. And then he disappeared and it transpired that he had put the bookcase into storage for all those years." Armand couldn't believe his luck as he set about acquiring this crown jewel. The excitement of the unique discovery is reflected in his face. "If I like one thing I follow it. I have an urge. It's not an urge to accumulate, it's an urge to find the best of its kind." And how Armand has dressed this bookcase is an education in style and discernment.

Well, time has rendered much of the impudence of Memphis into charm; and Armand's apartment, with its sophisticated interplay of paintings and furniture, has oodles of that and plenty of moxie. His iteration of a Big Bang furniture moment is alive with vitality and verve because of his rigor and reined-in creativity. And, of course, his unerring judgment.

ABOVE The grey walls and curved architecture – and Jennifer Guidi's huge sand painting – make the dining area a surprisingly calm background for those bright primary colors and graphic shapes. OPPOSITE, CLOCKWISE FROM TOP LEFT Beefburger beanbags from Urban Outfitters, under a painting by Amir Nikravan; through the alcove a painting by Joshua Nathanson. In a corner of the living room, an iconic floor lamp by Ettore Sottsass matched in color and verve by Maria Sanchez"s "Squash Ashtray," on a side table by Snarkitecture. More Memphis in the bedroom with a bedspread of Sottsass fabric and lamp by George Sowden; the painting is by Ryan Trecartin and Lizzie Fitch. A glass sculpture by Flavie Audi on a coffee table by Peter Shire.

BRIO IN BLUE & WHITE

FRIEDERIKE KEMP BIGGS

Nothing prepares you for walking into Friederike Kemp Biggs's penthouse apartment atop a Rosario Candela building on the Upper East Side. (The buildings this Sicilian-American architect designed in the 1920s are among the most coveted in Manhattan.) She is a decorator and designer with electric energy and a gift for making those around her feel special, and she lives in a delectable series of rooms all of her own devising and crammed with pretty things.

So where to start . . . think of the condition of *amor vacui*, the love of empty space, the white box, detachment, minimalism, the lack of the impress of human personality. Then think the reverse. Luxury and romance. Expressiveness. Warmth and sensuousness – curves, fringes, furbelows, fabulous passementerie, loops, papier mâché, tole, painted panelling, painted wallcoverings. Think French Empire mixed with English country with New York panache, all done with a twist of exuberance, but most of all think blue and white – and now you're in Friederike's apartment, in an unrestrained but impeccable melange. The eye becomes inebriated as one totters from room to room, from congenial library to seductive drawing room to a kitchen that is unlike any other – black yet gleaming, highlighted by part of her collection of blue and white porcelain and ceramics – Delft, Spode, nineteenth-century Chinese export vases, as well as anything that takes her fancy. And Friederike is fancy.

She was born in Germany but has been an East Sider for many years – well before she moved here with her husband, Jeremy Biggs, an Anglophile and an investment manager. In 1958 they decided that they did not want to go to the country every weekend and thought a penthouse with a garden and a terrace would be a good answer. And this is the very thing plus a panoramic view. (Not that it precluded the country – there is also a fantastic house on Martha's Vineyard.)

Perhaps the dynamic that precipitously drives her – and she is a whirlwind of energy – to create such a *gemütlich* and soothing apartment is the fact that her parents were always on the move. "That's what made me want to create interiors that might last."

Although they loved the new apartment, major reconstruction lay ahead and since the building board regulations only allowed heavy construction from May to September (an atavistic rule dating from the epoch when every Upper East Sider worth the name departed New York for the summer months), it took more than two summer work sessions to do everything. "And we did do everything," Friederike says. "It was a total gut job. George Sweeney was our architect. We opened rooms and closed passages, added a powder room, bought an extra bit of terrace to make a larder."

The work went on. And on. "We raised the roof of the kitchen and knocked out the little elevator foyer so that you enter the apartment the minute you are off the lift and see the French doors to the terrace straight ahead – and the Empire State Building! We knocked the staff room and bathroom together and raised the ceilings to make my office." There was just one small high window in there so they had it reconfigured to make the handsome window with its clever mirrored reveals and big fanlight. Now the light streams in and she looks out on the wraparound terrace. It's quite unlike any other office I've ever seen – and certainly one of the prettiest - but she carries on her interior design business efficiently from within its unofficial charm.

Friederike had no knowledge of interior decorating - or indeed of business - when she started, but she had and has a natural talent for making a room look lovely, and she had learned how to sew from her mother. "When we were living in Formosa my parents took a weekend trip to Hong Kong, leaving me with the household help. I had a dress that I'd heard my mother say was too small for me, so I took it apart and made myself a pair of pedal pushers, which were most popular at the time. The zipper was a problem as I didn't have one – so I used snaps! When my mother saw what I had done she began to buy me patterns and fabrics and sewing became a part of my life. I never trained. It was totally my eye and the fact that I was actually able to sew."

And if she didn't sew everything herself she knew the techniques and how to get the best people and the best results. The elaborate curtains in her apartment, some of which look like something designed by Thomas Hope in the Regency period, others like Victorian lifted swags, were made by her upholsterer, an old European craftsman. "His name was Ernest and sadly he is no longer with us and I miss him."

Friederike uses blue and white in china and fabrics and objects as a highlighting motif in rooms where there is already plenty of pattern on pattern, and the end result is endearingly pretty. Her motto could be if there is an empty space – fill it. Yet it's not cluttered. Everything is spic and span, pristine in its detail, in its carpentry and coverings, in all its arrangements. She has an eye for proper spacing, the key to this kind of decoration. "I never buy anything unless I know I have a place for the object," she says and the mind reels at the inventory she must carry in her mind. "It is not easy to stop collecting or finishing a tabletop when one sees that perfect piece!"

Her dining room could be in a French chateau, but one owned by an unusually imaginative chatelaine. "The chandelier was bought in New York and I already had the dining room table and chairs before I married Jeremy – they have moved with me many times." (The chairs are English.) She's not above poking fun at the emphasis so often placed on provenance in her line of business. "The table?" she says, answering my query. "The table is Chipplewhite." She had the panels and cornice installed to give the room gravitas and the hand-painted wallpaper is by

the old New York/Chinese firm Gracie. (It puts one in mind of the lines by John Webster: "Tis just like a summer bird-cage in a garden: the birds that are without, despair to get in, and the birds that are within despair and are in a consumption for fear they shall never get out.") As in so many of her rooms, she positions mirrors to heighten and lengthen the dramatic effect.

The large peach-painted sitting room has a gilded Japanese screen along one wall and the others are covered in close-hung pictures collected over many years. Among them is a painting by the British artist Paul Maze, who taught Winston Churchill painting. Friederike gave it to her late husband, who greatly admired Churchill. The Irish looking glass hangs high over the marble mantelpiece in such a way as to reflect both the room and the huge collection of plates and boxes and *objets de vertu* that she has tracked down over the years.

Next door is the quiet and donnish library designed by Friederike for Jeremy, who was an avid reader. There's a nice letter written by a Dr. Prujean in the seventeenth century, asking an architect for a library built for "conveniency and ornament." This would have answered. On the ceiling is a medallion inscribed with a quotation from Thomas Jefferson:

"I cannot live without my books." Many of these books are first editions and they include all of Churchill's works.

Friederike's bedroom, its walls covered with sprigged fabric, epitomizes her style and éclat. The built-in wardrobes, the black lacquer four-poster bed from Rose Tarlow and the comfortable Victorian chairs covered in Brunschwig fabric – have become the architecture of the room.

In her kitchen she reversed the given rule that kitchens are bright and clinical – this is an exercise in brio, a luxurious riot of walls with a rubbed finish of black over Chinese blue limned in gold, of copper, china and enamel; but food is taken seriously here – witness the professional cooker. Friederike has dinner parties for up to forty people. And guess what? Willow-pattern plates and side platters of all hues – as long as they are blue and white – emblazon the kitchen. "Why, Friederike?" I cry, "Why," looking into her bright blue eyes

"The love for blue and white is revisited from my childhood," she says. "I had blond hair, usually with braids and blue ribbons. I often dressed in blue. And then the time came for me to outgrow this period. But now I am back in the fold – perhaps the circle is closing!"

ABOVE In the dining room, the chinoiserie wallpaper by Gracie is echoed by the Lee Jofa fabric covering the wing chairs. The dining chairs are English and Friederike calls the mahogany table "Chipplewhite." OPPOSITE The view through from the entrance hall to the large sitting room with its Regency chairs and an antique Japanese screen on the left-hand wall. The sofa in the hall on the right is known as a courting bench: it has a peephole to catch anyone daring to flirt. The hanging light came from Vaughan's in London.

It's an archetypal New York loft and it's not. For a start it seems more vertical than lateral, although it is wide, with cast-iron columns on the facade. It's been transformed ("adaptive reuse," in more formal terms) from an 1860s shoe factory in the heart of Tribeca, into a Live Work (and Play) loft.

It's organized on three levels, with architectural practice offices at front ground level and living spaces at the back tumbling downwards to the small terraced garden. Behind the secretive facade the loft – never reaching the top stories – soars up here, down there, in a wizard series of spaces; rooms loom over rooms in a sort of stratigraphy. When you peer over a cantilevered balcony down vertiginous spaces to the bottom floor – originally the basement, now the living room - and look outwards through the glass wall that constitutes the back of the building, you know that you are in a domestic and professional building inscripted, top to toe, by the sensibilities and skills of the architects who live here: Sandro Marpillero and Linda Pollak, the husband and wife team of the architectural firm MPA.

In their practice they pay heed to any given site's existing conditions and its history, and since they moved to this ramshackle previously industrial building in Duane Street in 2000 they have made real sense of refiguring it for the everyday necessities of living and working, while showing sensitivity to the physical experience of its interior and its rough history.

They are busy architects taking on big challenges; their work is done here in the book-lined and scale-model-filled offices at the front, and their output includes urban design and architectural projects in the United States, Italy and Japan.

Linda co-authored the award-winning book *Inside Outside: Between Architecture and Landscape*, exploring connections between architecture, country and urban landscape and the needs of clients, and has received fellowships from the American Academy in Rome, Harvard and the Design Trust.

Sandro has written the monograph Environmental Refractions on the architect James Carpenter, lectures in architecture and urban design at Columbia University, and has led design studios at Harvard, Yale and Princeton, and the Institute of Architecture in Venice (among others).

One of their latest projects is the $39.5 million, 21,500 square foot renovated Elmhurst Public Library in the borough of Queens. "We've had a lot of projects in Queens, mainly because of former mayor Michael Bloomberg - a visionary who directed his gaze outwards from Manhattan and donated huge amounts of money from his foundation towards the development of art and culture in places which had been long neglected."

Essential to their design philosophy is the distinctive use of natural light, and there is evidence of that in these multiple levels of spatial complexity – what could be a dark center in the building is alive with light under a long white ceiling.

They wanted neither pristine nor concealment anywhere, and the reuse of existing elements and preservation of the masonry walls played a key (and expensive) part in the aesthetics and narrative of the design. There's nothing whimsical here, nor vintage for the sake of it - the reconfiguration has been carried out with care and precise planning. The stairs are made from wood reclaimed from the original structure and the bricks and recycled rough wooden beams were cleaned by hand, as sandblasting would have removed the patina. "It's not recycling," Linda says. "It's upcycling. We don't sentimentalize the history of the house – we just respect it. It's challenging for every room to be part of a whole space and also to be its own space. We had Ecuadorian woodworkers who could do anything, anything with wood . . . the basins set into old beams, and the beds made from beams – they did it all. The idea of the beams was to wrap the old and the new. The house took a year and a half to build. When 9/11 happened we had to stop right in the middle of construction. The workers weren't allowed to come down here because of the pollution."

When I walked into their soaring space for the first time, along the narrow entrance hall, lined with the original brickwork, down the steep planked steps I thought somehow I had seen it all before, and then realized it was a prototype for so many ideas and practices – the natural light, the mixture of grainy original textures, the terracotta-colored old brickwork, the high-piled rooms, the use of space as an artifact, the deceiving sense of simplicity. All of it, of course, married to high tech. "Architects are pretty bad at interiors," Linda says, disarmingly, but Sandro did all the engineering in the loft and Linda's color sense and her love of textiles make for an integrated, unpretentious working and domestic space with an air of vibrating possibility.

This urban building linked into its dense city street connects via its glass wall with a deep terrace, created from an unpromising basement yard. On the dark garden wall opposite angled colored strips and ribbons of Plexiglas mirrors illuminate inside and out. "Coming down the stairs you can see the sky reflected in them and at night the mirrors turn dark blue and gold."

Linda likes pieces that have a powerful nature-ish persona – "not looking 'natural' per se – more like an eruption of nature." So their kitchen table is a cut of marble which, after use, swivels inwards to make an integrated unit; and the oxidized metal doors mottled with age cloaking the larders and storage cupboards were adapted by Sandro from the original shutters.

This work and live space has warmth (their cat, Carrie, perched on the staircase to supervise, adds a homely touch) and in the living room with its reproduction Eileen Gray sofas, Le Corbusier/Charlotte Perriand classic "His and Hers" chaises and Noguchi table it's hard to believe that it is carved out of a lower-level space, so light and airy is the atmosphere. "Lifestyle," says Linda (or was it Sandro?), "is the understanding and appreciating of comfort as it takes place in a unique location." Quite.

So when people want to know what a New York loft and its lifestyle look like – why – have a look at this.

PAGES 92-93 The office, on the first floor at the front of the building, is a more public space than the rest of the house. The staircase up to the mezzanine is so magical – each step connected to the next by the lightest of struts and almost invisibly supported on the bookcase – that it seems to float in the air. OPPOSITE The living room, with its reproduction Eileen Gray sofa, Le Corbusier/Perriand chaise longue and Noguchi table, seen from high up in the mezzanine library space, with the little courtyard garden beyond. The rows of wooden joists on the left and joist pockets on the right make visible where part of the first floor was removed.

OPPOSITE, ABOVE In the kitchen, the salvaged marble counter can swivel outwards to make a table; the oxidized metal pantry doors on the left were originally shutters. The white vases above the counter are a mix of Rosenthal Studio line, mostly from the 1960s, by Jonathan Adler, Ted Muehling and others. OPPOSITE, BELOW The new glass window and door at the corner of the bedroom bring in light from the east. The bed, bedside drawer and window frames were made from salvaged beams. ABOVE Steps up from the original ground floor go to the library, passing the private spaces of the living area, including the bathroom, closets and, further on, the bedroom.

ABOVE Carrie the cat surveys her territory. Stairs and shelving provide structure and define living and working areas. The vast bookcase houses art books; oversized books and journals are stored in mobile cases with foam rubber tops that can be pulled out for seats. OPPOSITE The original brick masonry wall runs from front to back and top to bottom of the building, providing a continuous calm backdrop. The stairs are made from salvaged wooden beams that originally supported part of the ground floor.

STRANGE PLACES CRAMM'D

UGO RONDINONE

The story begins. A Swiss-born American artist with an international reputation and an urgent, resilient and instinctive desire to make art is driving around Upper Manhattan in 2011 when, in the heart of Harlem, he sees – and he is a fierce seer in both senses – the vaguely Romanesque-style Mount Moriah Baptist Church, once a great gospel center but now badly needing restoration, with a For Sale sign up front. The last thing this artist needs is another house: he already has a loft on Broadway in the East Village and another place somewhere else and also has a diary full of commitments for intricate exhibition projects all over the world. So what does he do? He resists the siren call of the 15,500-square-foot monumental former church, puts pedal to the metal and drives on and away.

Three weeks later the artist, Ugo Rondinone, is lured back by his second sight, and takes another long look at the enormous building, now standing desolate. Reader, he buys it.

What he had let himself in for turned out to be a massive restoration job, far bigger than he had envisaged, but with his spectacular verve, nerve, massive energy and creative strategy he has turned this relic into a thriving sanctuary of art, divided into living and working quarters on a grand scale, its palatial interior lit by high stained-glass windows. It's now his main residence, his live, work and play place for the making of his own work, for planning the exhibitions of that work, for the exhibitions he curates all over the world and also for the exhibitions of other artists' work. To add to the general mash-up of cultural production the basement has smaller studios for a rotating cast of visiting artists of diverse disciplines.

Eighty per cent of his work is produced here in this building. There are ten people in the studios and in his office and he is very hands-on. In one room the architectural models that he has made to render what and how he wants everything to look, in the galleries and museums that will show his work, are miniature works of art in themselves. He is almost brisk in his perfectionism, and every proposal, what he conceives and places in these models, is exactly how the finished work will look. Not a centimeter out of place.

In the big chapel room is a startling installation of theatrical illusion – forty-five hyper-realist clowns, red noses and all, dressed in the colors of the rainbow (a recurrent emblem and motif in his work) are occupied, as it were, in sleeping, daydreaming, waking up, sitting, running, lying drooping or slumped. They are truly fantastical and are part of his solo show "The Vocabulary of Solitude" that opened in Rotterdam in 2016. These frighteningly lifelike wasted figures are not in any way comic. And their original function as commentators on life, like Lear's Fool, is hardly evident here – the traditional idea of a fool being a wise outsider with a cynical and melancholic eye has been exhausted out. The clown is a recurrent figure in Rondinone's work and appears in his performances,

installations, videos and sculptures, an archetypal example of how his work zigzags across the boundaries between fantasy and reality, despair and hope, autobiography and fiction.

Every room has a distinct function but the whole is satiated, saturated, instinctive with art, and so is Ugo Rondinone. "He's lovely," an artist friend warns me, "but he is very aggressive in his love of art." Indeed, art seems as necessary to Rondinone as oxygen is to the lungs. "I need art just to breathe," he says, simply and without pretension, and with no visible sign of aggression on his interested face. "It's an on-going spiritual experience – being surrounded by these people," he gestures towards the many people in the atelier, "and art energizes me. Art plays a lot with inherent forces that you don't see." He seems to be able to unpack the power of these forces. His vision, energy and fanatical purpose have crashed together like tectonic plates and just being inside this space, with its quasi-religious sensation of awe, its firework of echoes from wall to wall, makes one react to the immediate present or even to feel a little ahead of it. As he says himself, "Good art revolutionizes your whole being. It is something that stops you, or slows you down."

He works in a wide range of disciplines and media – installation, photography, sculpture, painting, sound, video and drawing, and it ranges from rugged and monumental and anthropomorphic to delicate and small. He also writes poetry. His works are in the collections of many museums and have been the subject of solo exhibitions at the Whitechapel Gallery in London, the Museum of Contemporary Art in Sydney, the Kunsthalle Vienna, the Musée d'Art Moderne, Centre Georges Pompidou in Paris, not to mention the intriguingly named Louisiana Museum of Modern Art in Humlebaek, Denmark. (Why is a museum in Denmark called Louisiana? Because the house that is now the museum was built by a Danish officer and Master of the Royal Hunt who married three women all named Louise.) Rondinone (with Urs Fischer) also represented Switzerland at the 2007 Venice Biennale.

The route to his eminence was not easy. He was born in 1964 to Italian parents in Brunnen in Switzerland, and might well have become an art teacher in a school there – that was, he says, the only feasible route open to a young working-class man trying to use his artistic gifts and talents, trying to fulfill his vocation and dream. "There were no schools dedicated to helping and educating young artists," he says, "though there were plenty of technology colleges and graphic and industrial design places – so, for people like the Giacometti brothers or Jean Tinguely the only option was to emigrate." "How can this be?" I ask him, astounded. "Perhaps it shows the formality of the Swiss mind," he says, smiling, and my mind hops back to Orson Welles and cuckoo clocks. In 1983 he had the opportunity to go to Vienna to work with Hermann Nitsch, the Austrian avant-garde artist,

The glowing night-time facade of the former Harlem Mount Moriah Baptist Church, built in 1887 and designed by architect Henry Franklin Kilburn, now a home, studio and exhibition space.

working in experimental and multimedia modes, and a year later he enrolled in the University of Applied Arts there.

In 1998 he moved to New York City and the energy of this city matches his rattling energy. He doesn't stop working since art is work and his work is his life. "I don't have family. I have time," he says simply. "Coming from my background as the child of immigrants, where you keep your head down, you do your best to fit in . . . you have to break out somehow? I needed freedom of expression, a contradictory form to break that pattern. There are two forces behind my work. The dynamic lies in creating opposites; for me it's the dynamics of Beckettian existence and German romanticism. And whenever I do something in white I have to do it in black. And the foundation of all my work is the natural world – that is the inspirational source."

So this old temple is a metaphor for his life and work – reaching towards the ideal, making a new meaning from the everyday and from the previous. But every rupture is also continuity; in its previous incarnation this place was a powerhouse for a different kind of belief, and that professing worship of something metaphysical and spiritual lives on.

And not just metaphysically speaking – physically it's a beautiful place now, especially when viewed from outside at night, lit up like a beacon of light and color.

Inside it may be a theatrical set dedicated to the great drama that is art, but it is also one man's illuminated domestic space. The main room is spectacularly high and one has to tilt back to squint up at the bizarre chandeliers, original to the building, as are the inset beams gleaming with gilt and color, banding the coved ceiling. The original but startlingly modern-looking stained glass windows, like three great round-headed rockets about to take off, are exemplifications of art installation in themselves and Ugo Rondinone looks out every morning from his bedroom (guarded by a recumbent Italian ceramic zebra that he has had for years) at the light they cast. "The windows face east so every season gives new patterns and different colors. Every morning the light changes the whole room. It's such a sacred place . . . filled with that kind of energy from down the ages."

Its shamanistic qualities are perhaps echoed in the scary oil painting hung over his bed – *Red Riding Hood & the Wolf*, by Verne Dawson, an archetypal work by this American artist who investigates the continuities that persist in human nature and ancient culture. Under the windows are a series of etchings in bright yellow acrylic frames by the painter, sculptor and installation artist Paul Thek, who died in 1988 – they seem almost like a touching memorial to him. Nearby stands *Bright Shiny Morning*, a tree sculpture in resin, a literal still life by Ugo Rondinone. (A quote from *As You Like It* arrives unbidden in my head – "He hath strange places cramm'd/With observation, the which he vents/In mangled forms." But nothing is mangled here. It's pure and stripped down.)

Above the arched entrance to his bedroom hangs *Amerika*, a big gold watercolor, book pages on linen made by the joint

Elegant Romanesque stained-glass windows illuminate the dining area and Ugo Rondinone's *Bright Shiny Morning* tree sculpture. On the wall to the left are two *Head* sculptures by Bruno Gironcoli and underneath the central window are twenty-eight etchings by Paul Thek. An Italian ceramic zebra lies by the chaise longue near to a 20th-century anonymously carved wooden dog (a bit of a rescue one).

altruistic enterprise Tim Rollins and K.O.S., Kids of Survival. (I get even more excited, as Tim Rollins and K.O.S. have worked for my husband in England, creating art for his foundation for deprived children.) One wall of his bathroom is a stained-glass representation of a bathroom by Urs Fischer; in fact it's a perceptual trick that works on many levels, being a meticulous and witty reflection of the real bathroom.

There are other stained-glass windows hidden behind walls to give more space for display, and sculptures and installations stand in carefully curated spaces. But nothing is fixed — you don't step twice in the same river here. New work arrives often and things are rehung and rearranged. His collection has expanded and is wide ranging. He began by collecting Swiss artists in the early 1990s: "Now 60 per cent

of the works in my collection are exchanges with other artists who are my friends."

On Mondays, Wednesdays and Fridays he has lunches and get-togethers. "Who for? I ask. "Friends? Curators? Art critics? Writers? Artists?" "All of that," he says. "And people who happen to be passing by?" "No one passes by here," he says, smiling. I've forgotten that though he lives on Fifth Avenue he's very far uptown, in every sense.

I think if one were asked by an alien culture to make a template to show an energizing example of contemporary art, to convey what its place of creation could look like, to deliver an idea of our strange and mysterious culture, of how artists haul the lyre up in the face of the gods of the underworld, this might well be the place to start.

OPPOSITE A curtained archway into the bedroom shows Verne Dawson's *Red Riding Hood & the Wolf*. Above is *Amerika* and to its right *The Birds II* and *A Journal of the Plague Year*, all by Tim Rollins and K.O.S. Next to the bathroom stained-glass piece, Martin Boyce's chair sculpture, *Anatomy (for Saul Bass)* sits below Verne Dawson's *Coronation*. ABOVE Urs Fischer's stained-glass representation of Ugo Rondinone's bathroom, seen here from the bathroom side, is illuminated by the light in the living room.

The huge, light-filled living and dining space. On the wall below the coving is *Single Swing Encounter* by Alan Shields hanging over Valentin Carron's cross sculpture, *I Miss the 20th Century*. Above the fireplace stands Ugo Rondinone's *The Tactful* and in front of it Sarah Lucas's *Obod Daddy 2*. The chairs are by Franz West.

A DANDY PLACE TO LIVE

HAMISH BOWLES

Although nothing could be further from the cork-lined bedroom on the Boulevard Haussmann in Paris where Proust lay obsessively writing his masterpiece, Hamish Bowles's apartment near University Place in New York is as evocative of past time as any dipped madeleine. There might well be a slippered Céleste figure in the background, straightening Master Hamish's monogrammed slippers, folding that cerise dressing gown and placing the little vase of muguet on his bedside bureau – rather than the reality of his yet again packing a suitcase (an aesthetic education in itself, never mind its bonsai-compression aspects) for another foray into the teeming international world in which he lives.

So who is Hamish and what is he, that all his friends commend him? He is atavistic, modern, isolated, sociable, a scholar, a dandy, an aesthete, an obsessive collector, a balletomane, a writer, a curator, a darling of fashion. He has been a peripatetic International Editor at Large on American *Vogue* for over twenty years. He is much loved by a great many people, gossiped about, speculated on, knows everyone and everyone claims to know him. (Gentle reader, you know what I mean by everyone.) Where he lives is at the center of his life. Everything in it matters. Every vision. Every detail. Every flounce. Every color, especially purple and lavender, although his prose – he writes beautifully – eschews the color (I can't). Here are some of the things written or said about him and/or his apartment: "Eclectic but classical in feeing . . . Quirky neoclassicism . . . Fastidious taste . . . A certain amount of disdain . . . A breadth of culture."

He was born and raised in England but there has never been anyone more suited to being called a citizen of the world than Hamish. "When I was a little boy my mum was obsessed with junk and antiques and I used to go with her and buy what I could afford with my pocket money. I was a solitary child, a funny mixture, and I had my own world entirely unrelated to the things my fellow schoolboys were interested in." (I'll say! He painted his boyhood bedroom a blushing-apple pink and hung reproduction Mucha posters and fabulous 1920s *Vogue* covers on the walls.) "So I was a real fish out of water, and my friends' mothers thought I was a pernicious influence. I retreated into my own world and began collecting vintage fashion and haute couture. Christie's South Kensington had started their costume and textile sales – so I skipped class, failed my French but acquired some marvellous things. I've just gone on collecting. I have three thousand pieces in storage now. It's like an autobiographical collection."

Frustrated at school, he took matters into those fine-grained hands of his and secretly put together a portfolio of his fashion drawings for St Martin's School of Art. He was accepted, was soon noticed by the editors of fashion bibles and began working at *Harper's Bazaar*. "Then Anna Wintour called for an interview for British Vogue and off I went in a Chanel jacket with a Chanel handbag insouciantly flung over the shoulder – that's what I happened to be wearing at the time. I shudder to recall. Needless to say, I didn't get the job."

PAGES 108–109 On the *verre églomisé* top of a Charles X table found in the Clignancourt flea market, gifts from friends include a paperweight from Albert Hadley, an early 19th-century terracotta box from Allegra Hicks, a surrealist eye from Allison Sarofim, and a Georgian salt from Gordon Watson. OPPOSITE Studio Peregalli designed the gessoed library panelling and the green and gold paper frieze. The 18th-century mirror is flanked with pictures by (left) Martin Battersby, Philippe Jullian and Violet, Duchess of Rutland, and (right) Lawrence Mynott, Marcel Vertès and Pierre Le-Tan.

PAGES 112–113 The Récamier sofa in the center of the library drawing room came from a scheme by the American decorator Sister Parish. Studio Peregalli covered it in custom-dyed marmalade silk velvet. On the left are a marble-top Louis XV table, a white-painted needlepoint Louis XV *bergère* chair and a 1850s gesso slipper chair upholstered in lilac watered silk. The 1961 portrait of the Queen is by Alfred Kingsley Lawrence, and the obelisk bookcase is an early David Hicks design – its coloring exactly matched the scheme chosen for the library. The mid-18th-century etchings hanging on the frieze above the panelling are by Charles Nicholas Cochin. ABOVE In the entrance hall the walls are hung with cotton moiré found at Alef in Cairo. The Louis XV side chair was upholstered in leopard-stamped pony skin by designer Albert Hadley, and the leopard trench coat is by Saint Laurent. On the Charles X table the lilac column lamp is crowned with a lampshade made by Studio Peregalli of antique sari fabric. Behind it is a late 1940s fashion study by Carl Erickson (Eric), and above hangs a portrait of Mozart by Eugene Berman. Above the chair is a sketch by Glyn Philpot and on the kitchen's jib door is a Cecil Beaton drawing of Queen Ena of Spain. OPPOSITE, CLOCKWISE FROM TOP LEFT On the William IV console table is a 1930s Constance Spry vase and a bust of Noel Coward by his stage designer, artist Gladys Calthrop; the Regency pier glass is flanked by a self-portrait by Violet, Duchess of Rutland and her portrait of her daughter, Lady Diana Cooper. Aubusson tapestry upholstery on a Louis XV side chair and on the drawing room sofa Le Manach's Palmyre fabric, finished with silk fringe custom-made and dyed by Studio Peregalli. 19th-century encaustic floor tiles from Valencia, and Lee Jofa's hand-blocked Kingston Lacy chintz shower curtain in the main bathroom; the *trompe l'œil* painting above the lavatory is by Martin Battersby. In the bedroom, a portrait of Truman Capote by René Bouché, used for the dust jacket of the paperback edition of *Breakfast at Tiffany's*, hangs below an Augustus John nude.

He is wonderfully funny and self-deprecating. When he recently visited a fanciful little palazzo in Sicily, he "just about fainted clean away in each new room."

I could easily have a fainting fit or, in an archetypally Hamish phrase, *je die* when I enter his apartment, which lies like a tiny Atlantis in a 1920s building in Greenwich Village. Lo, sesame! Through a door tucked into a far first floor corner, one is transported into a magical domain, each room illuminating Hamish's meticulous, obsessive attention to the cut and construction of his life. You dive into purple in a lobby hung in a buddleia-mauve moiré fabric he found made up in jackets at Atlas Silks in the Cairene souk. He sought out the source —as any halfway normal person might— at Alef in Zamalek, as it happens, but boldly went where no man had gone before and bought the entire stock. It now covers the walls as well as his body, walls crowded with close-hung prints and drawings, above a Louis XV chair upholstered by Albert Hadley in leopard-patterned pony skin and two Queen Anne Revival chairs designed by Frances Elkins — that great 1930s decorator — flanking a William IV console. (Those chairs were the first things Hamish bought after he moved to New York.)

This little charmer leads into a gessoed book-lined library/drawing room that looks like the manifest of a dream, resonating with a rich dialogue of color and harmony hovering between lilac and the appropriate favorite imperial purple. It reminds me of the Camondo Museum in Paris and is a conceit of visual nostalgia, but not an incarnation of the past. It is the result of a collaboration between Hamish and the Milanese architecture and design firm Studio Peregalli, ruled by two wizards, Roberto Peregalli and Laura Sartori Rimini.

So how to sum up Studio Peregalli? For my money — and my! you need a lot — they are the best decorators in the world, the sole inheritors of the mantle of Renzo Mongiardino, perhaps the greatest of modern baroque decorators. When Roberto and Laura met he was studying philosophy and the decorative arts and she was an architect fascinated by old buildings.

Roberto's parents were friends of Mongiardino, so he was steeped in his ethos and aesthetic. The designers see his legacy as much more than an agglomeration of brilliant details. "He taught us to mix rigor with imagination," Peregalli says. Mongiardino's nostalgic rooms and romantic stage sets are mapped into their collective unconscious. (The first time I saw an example of his work was in Lee Radziwill's house near Oxford, decades ago; I was bowled over.) Studio Peregalli's superb artists and craftsmen bring their *coup d'œil* magic to palazzos and mini-palazzos all over the world. (Nothing as prosaic as the word house or apartment can contain their style; that witty cynosure Patrick Kinmonth — who once pronounced, succinctly and accurately, that decoration is a matter of biography — even coined the word "flatazzo" to describe Hamish's apartment.)

Seeing these rooms also reminds me on a miniature scale of Charles de Beistegui's extravagant Château de Groussay (fabulous is not too strong a word). Beistegui had been a fanatical modernist in the 1920s but he turned against the movement and proclaimed that minimalism was bourgeois. And indeed Hamish's apartment shows up the modernist, minimalist,

boring, tame sameness of so many New York apartments. Hardly anything fashioned after the First World War has made the cut. The place is padded and chintzed and painted and carved and stuffed with gilt and garniture and Louis XV furniture up to its pretty eyes. But his style has style — he knows how to play things right up and then to prick any pomposity by playing it right down. For example: a huge unicorn head rears in the broken pediment in his drawing room/library. "I found it in Oyster Bay on Long Island. I always loved unicorns and I love how it deflates the pomposity of the broken pediment."

Every room is crowded with the culmination of his discerning years of collecting, including *objets de vertu*, *objets trouvés*, books, drawings, pictures and recherché Louis XV and Louis XVI furniture which is, as he says, "bafflingly unfashionable." I shouldn't think it will be for much longer. (Oscar de La Renta gave him the moss-colored silk velvet that now upholsters a Louis XVI *bergère* stamped Jacob.)

It is a romantic interior in the true sense — defined not only as a stylistic term but also by the character of the objects it contains and by the motives of its creators. His motives include creating a Hamish cosmology. In his drawing room and in his dressing room are portraits of himself taken or painted by friends over the last thirty years . . . "and a proper rogue's gallery it is."

It could all give a minimalist a panic attack, but it shows the knowledge, taste and relish of a cultivated and refined man. It's an apartment you can imagine the Comte de Mornay, or Cecil Beaton, or Madeleine Castaing finding ravishing. He discovered it seven years ago. "I was living in Sutton Place, which was perfect when I was working on the Jacqueline Kennedy show." (He curated "Jacqueline Kennedy: The White House Years" at the Metropolitan Museum of Art in 2001.) "But afterwards it felt a bit distant from things and I thought to move. Friends who had been house-hunting called to tell me of this apartment in a building I sort of knew about — it has attracted aesthetes through the years and was built for bachelor artists. A kitchen in the basement served the whole building — a dumb waiter threaded its way up through all the apartments. I have to say my heart skipped a beat when I saw it — it was the apartment of my dreams — talk about pomegranate possibilities!

"It belonged to a literary editor who had lived there for more than fifty years from 1957, and it was in an advanced state of decrepitude; she had not touched it for years. Festoons of wires looped everywhere and layers and layers of old greying net curtains. Sagging bookcases lined the walls and I found a window completely blocked by bookshelves. There was a quaint Sunset Boulevard-ish wrought iron Juliet balcony opening into the main room. In a way it had a kind of appealing dowdiness and I had a plan in the works . . . there was going to be minimal architectural intervention . . . *Fâcheuse illusion!*" His voice trails away. "Then Studio Peregalli arrived. I had known Roberto and Laura for years — but to employ them you have to be Maecenas. So when they said, 'What about us doing it as our American calling card . . .'" Hamish and I stare at each other open-mouthed. He nods. I say, channelling Shylock: "Thus ornament is but the guilèd shore to a most dangerous sea."

CALENDARIO
ALFABETO

OPPOSITE, CLOCKWISE FROM TOP LEFT The revolutionary staircase, built in 1975, which joined the kitchen to the studio. The vertiginous view over the studio (which was once used as a dance studio by Rita Hayworth). A storage space for canvases beside the staircase leading to the small studio. One of the stone mantels built and carved by Gonzalo with recesses for his pipes and for placing small found objects. ABOVE A painting by Caio hangs above a desk with two further small paintings by Gonzalo. The handsome lights are early American.

or South American, and the children didn't eat with the adults until they were older.

When they ate at that big old table, if they looked towards one wall they saw a fourteenth-century Chancay burial textile sewn together to make a tapestry as touching as anything out of Cluny. (Chancay was a Pre-Columbian archaeological culture, later part of the Inca Empire.) If they looked to the other side they saw many paintings by Gonzalo and, among other fine pieces, the polished granite body of a magnificent Egyptian sculpture standing beside carved African figures. They were warmed by a fire topped by a pile of building bricks that Gonzalo made for his children.

One particular significant space was already almost immutably there – the magnificent huge white studio. Isabel describes the room as "a silent, skylit painter's paradise soaring upward in 40-foot twin peaks, built 60 feet out on what would have been the back yard."

Their father labored in there and Isabel describes his way of working: "His studio on the first floor was his *sanctum sanctorum*, a separate country in a different time zone, as it seemed to us, guarded by a forbidding sentry in a glass case behind my father's desk in the studio's marginally less dusty anteroom. 'Uncle George,' as we called him, was a mummy from Papua New Guinea with shells for eyes and an apple-size shrunken head. Unlike my own children, who wander freely into both their parents' studies, we wouldn't have dared pass Uncle George."

Part of the house is dark, bookish, with the air of a reading room – and some of it is like an atelier, full of light. Every room in the house has its own particular history in the making of art, though the business of "making art" was not organized or taught. Art was just what the family did, and each one did it mostly on his or her own. They maneuvered their own way towards their art destinations, hunters and gatherers of values, bonded together in their foretime. An adolescent Bruno taught himself to draw, copying drawings by Old Masters and Cézanne; and in his room Caio also drew – mostly political cartoons for undaunted and unsuccessful submission to the *New Yorker*. Quina designed and made clothes on the dining table and, in her attic aerie that no one else climbed up to, Isabel wrote and illustrated stories. She is now a successful author, her works including the bestselling *Bury Me Standing: the Gypsies and their Journey*, about the lives of the Romany people.

When Elizabeth and Gonzalo separated and he moved out, the house changed again. She created a proper though fairly inaccessible studio of her own – a high-walled mezzanine loft at the back of the big room, reached only via a ladder and through a trap door, When in 1975 the writer and political activist Richard Cornuelle moved in, the configuration changed yet again. "It was a revelation," Isabel says, "like our own Berlin Wall coming down, when a new stairway was built to connect the studio to the kitchen and the space was cleared for parties. But as the parties wound down and the rest of us moved out, the essential setting remained intact – every chair, object, textile and child's lumpy clay creation secure in its appointed spot."

Now in the light-filled reservoir of air and space that is the studio turned living room, the talent of the family is made manifest - a big wonderful yellow canvas by Caio; a striking and impressive painting, *The Boy with a Column*, by Bruno, done in 1981; a memorable picture of an androgynous young figure with a dog lying on the floor painted by Elizabeth. "A work of imagination," Isabel says, "though also something of a self-portrait."

There's a painting by Horacio Torres, the other artist son of Joaquín Torres García. A comely stone French medieval madonna holds the Infant Jesus and both gaze down at the grand piano below them. An early American wooden articulated mannequin shows just how much the human body changes with every fashion epoch and on an easel nearby stands a big green 1961 painting by Gonzalo. On another wall hang several charcoal drawings by Caio. A kilim hangs over the high balcony studio, an old gilt French chair sits beside a junk shop find; we are in true bohemia, that much-sought-after territory, unselfconscious in its beauty, its slight disorder, its integrity and its understanding of what is serious.

But in bohemia one never knows what is going to happen next; the unexpected is part of the dream. The house has had a resurrection in a sort of reverse phoenix-like way. Quite recently there was a fire in the house in Brooklyn where Isabel, her husband, Martin Amis, and their two daughters, Fernanda and Clio, lived; and so, as Isabel says, "We have moved into the old house for the foreseeable future, restoring a waxy burnish to the floors and, we hope, lively conversation to the kitchen table. The beat goes on."

So the house is alive again, full of family life, rising and shining.

PAGES 126-127 A snapshot view into the myriad interests and creative activities of the Fonseca family, Many paintings by Gonzalo hang above a bookcase bearing African and Maori figures and masks, and a polished granite Egyptian torso. The bronze hand was a gift from the sculptor John Dann. The big table was made by Gonzalo from found pieces of wood, as were the small constructions on the wall and on the bookcase. On the sofa, a glimpse of a velvet appliqué cushion made by Quina for her mother. OPPOSITE, CLOCKWISE FROM TOP In the dining area, a polished granite sculpture stands near a construction piece by Gonzalo; on the wall a fourteenth-century Chancay burial textile sewn together to make a tapestry. The striking yellow exterior of the Fonseca house in Greenwich Village. A guest bedroom with the Peruvian Cuzco Madonna, dating from around 1750.

LIGHTHOUSE ON FIFTY-EIGHTH

MODULIGHTOR

When Rosamond Bernier, ancient cornerstone of New York artistic life (she died at the age of 100 in 2016), creator of the art magazine *L'Œil*, dazzling lecturer at the Metropolitan Museum of Art, friend of Picasso, Matisse, Joan Miró, Max Ernst, Georges Braque and Fernand Léger, was advised by the architect Philip Johnson, in his egocentric way, that, besides him, the only other two architects she should know about were Frank Lloyd Wright and Paul Rudolph she was astonished to think that she – who knew everything and everybody – hadn't heard of Rudolph.

Although he was hailed by historian Sibyl Moholy-Nagy as one of a handful of American architects who broke the Atlantic sound barrier, creating designs that were more than the sum of their European influences, and though some of the pioneering buildings he designed in the USA now have Landmark status, he is nothing like as well known as he should be. But he alienated many who disliked his frequent use of concrete, the new brutalist aspect of his buildings and his high modernist style – for all he spoke its language magically and brilliantly. (Le Corbusier, who held that the human body and hand is the perfect model of proportion and that everything should be designed to the human scale, gave Paul Rudolph a wooden model of his "open-hand" monument sculpture, in recognition.)

Rudolph's work and ideas are key elements in modernist architectural design. During his lifetime the style fell out of fashionable favor. Now, though, his reputation has undergone a dramatic rehabilitation. Late modernism has become an acknowledged historical style and Rudolph's buildings are recognized as an important part of American architecture of the twentieth century (not that that has stopped some of them being razed by philistine developers and myopic governments).

This most prodigious architectural talent of his generation was born in Kentucky and educated at Harvard, where he met Walter Gropius, the founding director of the Bauhaus. When Gropius was asked who were his most talented students he replied, "Paul Rudolph and I.M. Pei, in that order."

He was seminal in the establishment of the Sarasota School of architecture and as Dean of the Yale School of Architecture taught a generation of architects. Norman Foster, one of his students, has credited him with being the most important influence in his life.

And here in New York, lighting up a side street in midtown Manhattan over by Second Avenue soars the Modulightor building, a fine and late example of Paul Rudolph's work, a light-filled jewel of a house, an artificial geode, so conceptually integrated that when you're inside the outside world seems ready to invade. The building looks big, yet it is carved out of a 20-foot-wide townhouse-sized plot capsule, an effect magnified by its facade, a glass wall divided by white-painted steel elements into expanses of windows that advance and recede, brilliantly suggesting depth within shallow dimensions.

He is often compared to Frank Lloyd Wright, but where Lloyd Wright needed lateral space Rudolph here used vertical sky space, his ideas – and his building – spiraling upwards. With his customary passion and intense focus he had envisaged the whole building and overseen the first phase of its construction (from the first floor to the fourth) before his death from mesothelioma in 1997.

Later another architect who had worked for Rudolph and was familiar with his design DNA, so to speak, added two more floors and the roof deck. The deck made of subway grills filters light on to a skylight and the store below; in this vivacious place light is an essential element of design.

The building was planned initially to be multi-use; the Modulightor showroom on the first floor (with workshops below), Rudolph's office on the second floor and luxury duplexes above. Ernst Wagner, a delightful man, now lives in the third-floor duplex. He is a torchbearer for Paul Rudolph and is passionate about preserving his legacy; he was with him every step in this building and the setting up of the business within it.

"Modulightor was our creation. I knew Paul from 1974 onwards. He was a shy, lonely single man and we met socially and became friends and business partners. I had been an exchange student at Columbia University and was always interested in design . . . I was his 'student,' and he trained my eye. It was a very harmonious friendship. He was the most considerate person I ever met and full of *joie de vivre*.

"In the late 1980s our offices' leases were both up and he became interested in our owning a building together and setting up here, his architectural office on the second floor and the Modulightor on the first. And then, too, the modernist style of architecture had become very unfashionable and he had time on his hands. So we set out to find a house for rentals and the showrooms and his architectural offices, and of course we had to see if the thing was financially feasible. Money was always tight and New York costs always expensive.

"We found a nondescript commercial four-story wood structure on East 58th Street. We didn't know that it had originally been a steel structure, and we got wrong advice from an expeditor who didn't tell us that if you make radical changes to a 'grandfathered' commercial building it reverts back to its original zoning as a mixed-use building. So the wood structure had to be dismantled – every piece, beam by beam, pulled out and replaced with steel. And it was also the wrong time. We bought it in 1988, at the top of the market, for $1.7 million. Two years later the building next door was sold for $750,000.

"When he was designing and building the house Paul would meet with the workers in the morning and – like a sculptor – have them make countless mock-ups of the kitchen cabinets, and built-in furniture with foam boards, adjusting and balancing the forms with the voids until he was satisfied. He was always experimenting with the latest developments in technology and new materials. He designed every square inch of the building and there is no wasted space in the showroom or the house. At one point I asked him, 'Isn't it going to be too complicated?' He replied, 'You don't understand! Architecture is like music. Do you think a Bach fugue is too complicated?'"

PAGES 130–131 A view of the third-floor living room (the lower level of the duplex) with the whole interior, including chairs and tables, designed by Paul Rudolph. The apartment is richly planted, as Rudolph always envisaged. OPPOSITE A fitted seating area under floating steps to the mezzanine. The versatile modular shelving serves as both library shelves and spaces for the display of objects. PAGE 134 The building seems to rise effortlessly from a relatively narrow (20-foot-wide) plot on 58th Street, the pale geometric lines making this north facade light but mysterious. PAGE 135 Looking through the living room towards the south terrace. The shelving and stairs seem to hover in space, the flashes of green from the planting accentuating the airy, other-worldly atmosphere.

PLEASE WATCH
YOUR STEP

Everything was a series of on-site sculptural experiments, and the precise, economical way he integrated everything here – bathrooms, bedrooms, kitchen, a place for his Steinway, outside terraces and living spaces – may owe something to his training as a naval architect in Brooklyn's Navy yards during the war.

The Modulightor is still a radical design and would seem to challenge the rules of the New York building code. At the time they bought it zoning laws allowed a nine-story structure but even with the change in zoning laws bringing it down to six stories it looks like a latter-day ivory tower such as a digitalized Rapunzel might dream in, or a runic structure left behind after an early moon launch attempt, so vertically and pristine does it rise from prosaic East 58th Street.

Ernst says, "Everything – the engineering, the air-conditioning, every door knob – all was part of the architecture. He would see a wall of graffiti or a decaying building and he would see beauty; he would use what he saw and was moved by. We are all artists, gifted or not, and are influenced by things we see. For Paul it was Greek art. When he saw the Acropolis for the first time early one morning as the sun was hitting the Doric columns – it was a moment of such beauty. And later this was the impulse for his famous ribbon-fluted concrete – like corduroy – copied in so many ways all over the world."

This pioneering architect always had an extraordinary way with floating planes within an interior, and his ideas were faithfully carried out here.

They re-created the design for shelving which Paul Rudolph had originally made for his Beekman Place apartment – shelving which is such a talismanic part of the transparent interior here. Multi-level walkways and cantilevered stairs lead to different levels, different elevations and suspended spaces in a complex layered design – all of which doesn't altogether make a template for a comfortable design for domestic living (one dreads to hear the patter of tiny feet tumbling down the delicate sequence of floating steps), but otherwise it works well, and – almost literally - like a dream. The whole thing is, paradoxically, a vision of invisibility anchored by greenery and objects and an awareness of the outside world behind glimmering glass. It is empirical proof of Paul Rudolph's tenet that light is architecture's fourth dimension. (He even deployed storage as part of his transparent architecture – using ranks of wine glasses on suspended shelves as a shimmering kitchen divider for example.)

An elevator zooms from floor to floor – the floors are covered with Berber rugs adding vivid color – and although one might never be quite sure which level one is walking on to, each one is full of many ingenious and delightful toys, masks, important aboriginal pieces, ethnic hangings, indigenous objects, antique tools, feathered headdresses from Peru, ancient miniature heads, hundreds of Moroccan flax combs and vintage agricultural items like tractor seats and camshafts that Paul and Ernst collected wherever they travelled – literally *objets trouvés*. "He always felt architecture needed objects for enrichment," Ernst says. Well, he certainly fulfilled that need here. There is a multitude of milagros – those little silver votive charms depicting a request for a miracle to be performed, or as a thanksgiving.

"He saw them being sold in the flea market of Mexico City for a few cents each and bought quantities of them." And there are the many little Roman heads from Sicily – "Fishermen of earlier times obtained these female statuettes and it was considered good luck if you broke the head off and threw it into the village well before setting sail. Every village had these heads," says Ernst, who is a dandy collector himself. (From an early age when he was growing up on a farm in Switzerland he collected old tools and anything that took his fancy. "It drove my family mad," he says, happily.)

There are early models of transformer robots in merry colors – all painted by Paul Rudolph on Sunday afternoons. Best of all, perhaps, are the scores of little twisted wire bicycles parked in baby rows on built-in recessed shelves in the elevator – almost like a glittering vitrine in a jeweller's shop – which were made by a man selling them on the street in London. Over the years Paul Rudolph bought as many as he could, until the man vanished. A small maquette of a monumental sculpture by Picasso, intended to be used in the Plaza of the University of Florida (but never built) makes a punctuation point along one of the glimmering ways of the house. Paul Rudolph liked the sculpture so much that he inquired about the possibility of getting a copy. Picasso arranged for one to be made for him by an authorized atelier.

And then there's the glory of the rich and rampant vegetation, ferns and vines spilling over the pristine planes of glass and Perspex, looked after by Eva (housekeeper for the past eighteen years, who seems to have the greenest fingers ever).

For Paul Rudolph light was a matter of fact; he thought of space as a material and was one of the creators of the concept that lighting should be wholly integrated with the architectural and interior design. Furniture too, he believed, should be an integral part of design and his modular chairs – inspired by watching Ernst working with aluminum modules and Plexiglas – are going into production (now in stainless steel, for strength). They are perfect in this space: indeed, every inch of this complex and dazzling house – dazzling in its true sense – illustrates Paul Rudolph's tenets.

Years before, Ernst had met Alberto Giacometti. "Paul reminded me in many ways of Alberto," Ernst says. "I met him in about 1962, in Stampa, in Switzerland." Ernst and Paul visited Alberto's brother, Diego Giacometti, in Paris, in 1985. "I was fascinated by the modular nature of Diego's light fixtures, and asked if we could make similar designs for Modulightor. He was interested but said that we should contact his dealer in New York, Pierre Matisse (the son of Henri Matisse). Sadly, Diego died a few months later and nothing came of the project."

Ernst continues to run the Modulightor lighting business from the first-floor showroom, selling hundreds of the light fixtures and lighting systems that he and Paul Rudolph designed. Many of the pieces sold in the showroom are fabricated on the three levels below, constituting another to-be-cherished rarity – since it's one of the rare remaining small artisans' workshops in Manhattan.

"For me, being here in the space is an experience of living in a sculpture, in a work of art," Ernst says. "Wherever you move you see other new fresh energizing and visual aspects."

Combining the practical and the aesthetic, suspended shelving for storing glassware creates the appearance of a shimmering glass curtain dividing the kitchen space.

OPPOSITE, CLOCKWISE FROM TOP LEFT Le Corbusier himself gave Rudolph this miniature of his symbolic sculpture *Open Hand*. Floating steps up to a bedroom and down to a living area with Rudolph's own grand piano. Modular shelving displays an idiosyncratic selection of objects collected by Ernst Wagner during his world travels. ABOVE The dining area with Rudolph's wheeled – and hence easily movable – versatile transparent acrylic and steel furniture, made from modular components.

After a joyous year of revolting,
the country fell into a serene slumber
that began with a picnic of ripe b...
guzzling Burgundy and stout,
one sated, sensuous, sozzled summer's
afternoon in about 1969 — and
it has never woken up.

The dining room and the sitting room were separate rooms with a supporting wall between but the Joe Serrins Studio people carved out two spaces so the rooms flow together. The wall between – Annie calls it her Yves Klein wall – is an installation in itself. It is indeed the exact blue associated with that artist. Annie and Russell sourced the paint from the Swiss firm KT Color, which mixes paints to reproduce in a non-toxic form the colors of such artists as Klein, Le Corbusier and Luis Barragán. All the details here are so considered.

So now a big space with windows on two sides is smoothly divided with, on one side, a combination of living room and a big working kitchen, with countertops made from white Corian and butcher blocks, Formica aplenty and penny tiles (so called because they are ¾ inch in diameter, like the standard penny); on the other side, the dining area, with its green opaline glass chandelier found at the much-mourned flea market down on 26th and

6th Avenue, is hung with paintings, photographs and texts. One piece, "ELEVEN ELEVEN ELEVEN," is by the celebrated British designer, and sorceress of color, Marianna Kennedy.

Every room glows with color – spring yellows, purple, blue – and pink blinds in book cloth cast a luminous glow over it all. Just look at the American sofa in the sitting room which Annie inherited from her grandmother. She had it upholstered in a Kenzo fabric in the bravest, pinkest pink, and piled it with kaleidoscopic cushions she made herself.

Their apartment overlooks frantic Lexington Avenue and looking out I remember Nora Ephron's little hymn: "I look out the window and I see the lights and the skyline and the people on the street rushing around looking for action, love, and the world's greatest chocolate chip cookies, and my heart does a little dance." And my heart does a little dance in here in this forthright world these artists have made their own.

OPPOSITE, CLOCKWISE FROM TOP In the kitchen, designed by Joe Serrins, Annie and Russell chose the glowing yellow and white of the Formica cabinets and the blue penny-tile splashback; the monochrome photograph of a pear tree is by Annie, and the woodcut portrait in the hall is by Nancy Loeber. A pink resin lamp with a bright yellow shade, by Marianna Kennedy, stands in front of Herman Miller bookshelves bought by Annie's parents in the 1970s; the oversized yellow-green jack on the floor was inherited from her grandfather; a cushion pigeon sits on another dumpster-rescue chair, now reupholstered in Designers Guild fabric. Russell designed the snaking tile pattern in the bathroom. ABOVE Jewel-like fabric by Kenzo covers a sofa that lived with Annie's grandparents for forty-five years. Annie took the Pantheon photograph early one morning, just before the Roman *carabinieri* noticed the unpermitted tripod. Beside it are two small gouache portraits studies by Nancy Loeber.

SILK STOCKING ASCENDANCY

LOUISE GRUNWALD

One of the most warming quotes I know about what and where home is comes from Henry Grunwald, editor-in-chief of *Time* magazine in its great heyday and, in the latter part of his life, with his beautiful wife, Louise, the US Ambassador to Austria. "Home is the wallpaper above the bed, the family dinner table, the church bells in the morning, the bruised shins of the playground, the small fears that come with dusk, the streets and squares and monuments and shops that constitute one's first universe."

The streets and shops that constitute home to Louise Grunwald are on the chicer reaches of the Upper East Side (once dubbed the Silk Stocking district of New York). Over the course of her life – though she has always been thoroughly cosmopolitan and an inveterate traveller – she has lived within a few blocks of where she was born. Now her tranquil and pale apartment in a block designed by Rosario Candela overlooks the dazzling display of daffodils lining the center of Park Avenue in the spring and the tulips in their dance in early summer sunshine.

"As soon as you walk into Louise's apartment, you feel you've set foot in a place that's been designed to make people look – and sound – their best. There's a polish, comfort and worldliness about her rooms, and a promise of great conversation, that both relax and stimulate – and make you want to live up to the setting. That promise, by the way, is always fulfilled. People do talk chez Louise, with a vigor and style that may surprise even the professional pundits among them." I didn't say that. Ben Brantley, the chief drama critic of the *New York Times* did – and he knows a fair amount about settings designed to make people sound and look their best. But I would echo it.

Here is a select mixture of comfort and worldliness and sophistication beyond sophistication that has somehow morphed into simplicity. But then simplicity isn't easy. So although this frankly grand, opulent apartment with its fine rooms and corridors, full of lovely things, could easily be stuck in a conventional time warp, it is animated by the spirit of its chic chatelaine, whip-sharp Louise, who knows how to spring a surprise or two. It is elegant – a rare quality in an interior – and it also has the American quality of freshness.

The paintings are remarkable, including a 1926 Picasso, worked in sand (and signed twice, for some reason) and a Hubert Robert painting of a building ablaze (he was sometimes called Robert des Ruines because of his romantic representations of Roman ruins, and this building is well on the way to becoming his favored subject); one could quite well be taken aback by the fiercely dominating painting *Irish Woman on a Bed* by Lucian Freud of a naked woman lying on a white bed.

Louise says, smiling, "A friend from London visited soon after I bought it, did a double take and said 'Oh! I know her!'" (The model, Cozette McCreery, now a fashion designer for her knitwear company, Sibling, was assistant to Bella Freud, Lucian's daughter, at the time; and looking at it one is reminded of Willem de Kooning's observation: "Flesh is the reason why oil painting was developed.") The painting is reflected in a *coup d'œil* in the eighteenth-century oval giltwood English looking glass; and on a table below is a Degas bronze of a girl precariously pulling

on her stockings. On a George III mahogany and gilt side table stands the handsome head of a Roman lady from around AD 200 and an alarming drawing by Bartolomeo Passerotti of the intertwined heads of two demons. I don't ask.

Many of the treasures in her apartment come from years of visits to flea markets, grand London antique shops and Long Island antique fairs, and from trips to the Middle East. Her first apartment was small, two bedrooms, in a rent-controlled building on East 66th Street. "I loved it." She was just starting out at *Vogue* and Diana Vreeland called Billy Baldwin, one of the great exponents of High Style, and asked as a big favor that he would decorate Louise's apartment for a minimal charge. "Anyway – he did it . . . and when it was about to be photographed for *Vogue* I called Diana Vreeland in a panic and asked her what I should wear – I had no money to buy anything grand. She said 'You've just been in Egypt – wear a caftan.'" Horst's photograph of Louise wearing a striped caftan became an iconic image in the sixties, and started a fashion.

Billy Baldwin produced a crisp, stylish, utterly American aesthetic and one that put comfort high on the agenda. She and he became fast friends. "When he took me on he said, 'What do you want to do now?' I said, 'I don't know.' 'Do you like English or French furniture?' 'I don't know.' He said, in frustration, 'Is there a house you like?' I said, 'I like La Fiorentina.' He said, 'Well, you've got taste.'" (La Fiorentina was the legendary villa on the tip of Cap Ferrat lived in by Lady Kenmare and her son Rory Cameron, who turned it into a spectacular magnet for luminaries and big cheeses from all over the world. Later Billy Baldwin decorated the villa for its new owners.) "I saw it when Lady Kenmare still lived there, after it was done up by Rory. I was about eighteen and my mother said, 'You must look around – look at every room, look at what is in it and see how out of every room there is another garden view.'" She looked, and learned about the importance of quality and perfection – and used the knowledge on every aspect of her life, including her appearance (she's on the International Best Dressed List Hall of Fame.)

She's witty and hits the nail on the head with precision. Talking about an early encounter with another great American decorator, Albert Hadley (and she has been described as "the model Hadley client"), she said, "There were a lot of boxes around . . . those were the days when we liked to have boxes." It summed up a vanished era of Boston ferns and Venetian boxes and I couldn't wait to scuttle home and remove my dated collection.

The simple linen slipcovers on the Louis XVI chairs in her salon hide exquisite original petit point embroidery. Because? "It's not the look I want now." (She allowed the chairs to be photographed without the slipcovers without fuss or demur; the same goes for the gleaming empty dinner table that I wanted to see piled with silver.) Comfortable modern chairs sit alongside grand French ones in harmony.

Her first place was the grand family townhouse originally built by Delano & Aldrich for the Cushing family and bought by her mother. "The things in it, though good, were not what would be my taste today.

PAGES 146–7 In the salon, on a George III mahogany table flanked by Louis XVI chairs, stand a Roman bust from AD 200, a drawing by Bartolomeo Passerotti of the intertwined heads of two demons and a 19th-century Viennese clock with the figure of a horse and rider. On the quarter hour the clock chimes and the rider's eyes move from side to side. OPPOSITE Lucian Freud's *Irish Woman on a Bed*, in the salon, overlooks a Degas bronze of a girl pulling on her stockings. On the side table, behind one of a pair of c.1770 George III chairs, a carved hand with furled fingers, bought in Damascus, sits alongside a 19th-century nude by Aristide Maillol.

"When I married Frederick Melhado he lived in a perfect apartment on East 72nd – like a little Irish house – and which had been done soup to nuts by Albert Hadley. My mother had died and I had inherited some nice furniture but there was only room for a pair of papier mâché chairs.

"We had to move a few years later because Frederick had two children and we needed more room. But it was 1973 and you couldn't give an apartment away in those days in New York. The first apartment I saw in this building was on the eighth floor, was HUGE - five master bedrooms - and cost $225,000! We bought it – and we lived in it for ten years. Marella Agnelli lived in this building then - well, it was her pied-à-terre, she used it for about a month a year - it was a 'little' apartment (by comparison) – and when I got divorced I asked her if I could buy it. Her husband's brother, Umberto, had to have first crack at it, but he didn't buy it and I moved here in 1986."

Naturally, Albert Hadley was on hand and he and Gary Hager of Parish Hadley helped her to turn it into the agreeable and charming place it is today. (The partnership between Sister Parish, as influential in American taste as Nancy Lancaster was in England, and Albert Hadley influenced interior decoration in the US for more than three decades.)

Soon afterwards she met Henry Grunwald at a party. They married three years later. An understatement to say that this meant certain changes. "For a start there were no bookcases. Can you imagine how many books Henry brought to this apartment? Combining his books and mine was like combining two armies." The bookcases in the morning room, one of the prettiest rooms in the house and really a library, were designed by Albert Hadley, as was the comfortable banquette above which hangs her collection of Old Master drawings. Louise had found a pair of Regency chairs for her bedroom and Parish Hadley made two copies indistinguishable from them – one sits at her William IV dressing table, a Waterford mirror above. Nearby is a nineteenth-century japanned bureau that was found by Sister Parish.

When Henry Grunwald was appointed US Ambassador to Austria Louise's life changed again. "The Viennese were thrilled to get a big deal as ambassador," Louise says, "and they wanted to claim him as a native son – but he was in every respect an American and very proud of it." It was a gratifying reversal – he had had to flee Vienna after the Anschluss and he came back to the city much lauded. She too was a brilliant success in Vienna and, for example, surprised the curators at the Kunsthistorisches Museum by how much she knew about – well – a whole lot of things. "I knew I had to acquit myself. I do my homework before I go someplace and I researched a lot and I had German lessons. We did everything together. I met more people in those two years in Vienna than in my whole life."

On the japanned bureau in her bedroom is a little model of a white bisque temple. "In my first week in Vienna I saw one just like this. I asked the price. I didn't buy it. Henry, of course, knew and loved the real temple, a small-scale replica of the Temple of Hephaestus in Athens, built in the nineteenth century and originally designed to house Canova's sculpture of Theseus in the center of the Volksgarten. I became friends with the curator of the Museum of Applied Arts and told him about it. He said, 'I know exactly what you are talking about - I bought it for the Museum!' Years later he calls me up. 'I've seen another model of the temple.' I bought it immediately."

She knows her antiques — she was once a partner in M. H. Stockroom Inc., a New York antiques shop — but insists that she is not a collector in the sense that many collectors are, intent on filling the psychic void. "I've collected paintings and pictures and sculptures over the years but I'm not a collector in the true sense."

You could have fooled me. Walking through the rooms and passages I see — among many other delectable things — a drawing of hands by Degas; a Louise Nevelson sculpture; drawings by Klimt; a covetable Hammershøi; two bisque busts of Austrian grandees (one of the Emperor Franz, the other of Prince Schwarzenberg); a painting of Haseley Court by Julian Barrow given to her by Albert Hadley; two handsome Regency paintings of different aspects of an English country house, possibly by Humphry Repton; a cache of David Roberts engravings of Egypt and Petra; an ancient Egyptian sculpture of a cat; a painting by Nicolas Lagneau, many antique Roman and Greek sculptures . . . no, obviously not a collector!

The dining room with its brown-lacquered walls is a *tour de force* – it took eight base coats to get the proper depth and finish. "The painter was not fancy at all – he was a house-painter, and he did it beautifully." Hanging above an eighteenth-century neoclassical console table with a St Anne marble top is a pair of paintings by Alexandre-François Desportes depicting Feast and Famine (symbolized by ham and oysters), and light bounces all over the place from a mirrored screen designed by Syrie Maugham. On the sideboard is a rare parade of a Chamberlain Worcester porcelain service.

The star of the room is a William IV circular expanding metamorphic table (it can have leaves added to make it larger), a Jupe table, made by the nineteenth-century English furniture makers Johnstone & Jeanes. She had seen one and wanted one. "I asked a good antiquaire I knew called Mr. Stair to find me one. And he found it! I bought it for £12,000." The set of magisterial nineteenth-century chairs, green tufted leather with a brass handrail, have a fascinating provenance too. Louise knew Nancy Lancaster - perhaps the most distinguished of all twentieth-century decorators, her work carried out with panache and throwaway elegance. "When I was still living at 72nd Street, Billy Baldwin told me about the sale of some of her furniture at Christie's. I particularly loved these chairs and went to bid on them. Christie's originally sold them in two lots of eight each. I bid on one lot and got them — with a faulty memory I recall spending $6,000. I had no place to put them then, so they went into storage. Over the years, I offered to buy the other set from Pamela Harriman, but she wanted mine as well. When I bid on them years later (and stopped at $75,000), I still had no place for them. I had two more made to match, so now I have a set of ten.

OPPOSITE An unnamed 1926 Picasso, done in sand, above the salon fireplace. On the mantelpiece, a terracotta Hercules wrestles the Nemean lion, in the first of his twelve labors. As well as the Degas bronze are figures including a gymnast by Barthélemy Prieur, and an Egyptian cat dating from around AD 200. The marble life-size female sculpture is Roman, 2nd or 1st century BC. PAGES 152–153 19th-century green leather chairs surround a William IV circular metamorphic Jupe table; the rare Chamberlain Worcester porcelain service was bought at Sotheby's. In the corner, a mirrored screen from Albert Hadley, designed by Syrie Maugham. On the wall is one of a pair of allegorical paintings by Alexandre-François Desportes.

Talk about! Susan Sheehan has opened the supply lines full torque, and these rooms now in their conception and realization, grandeur and spaciousness, their retaining treasures, spill out the past; but they're far from anachronistic follies – they are transformations and translations into a special visual language.

For a start the whole first floor was apartments, and on the third floor there were rent-controlled tenants who were not to be dislodged. They stayed for five years. But once they had gone she started in with unending relish on her quest and vision to restore the house and to be practical about it as well. ("We live on two of the five floors. The rest are my gallery offices and rentals.") The "we" is she and her husband, Irish-born John

O'Callaghan, now very much an American, with a worldwide custom carpet business.

Although John's impress and input is all over the house in its practical restoration and fanatical finish, he has, in Susan's words, "absolutely no interest in decoration." She says, with some amusement, "Once, when a guest asked him, when we had a benefit at the house, about the De Morgan tiles he told her that I'd bought all of it in China. But he is a great cook!" There would have to be great food in a house like this, which has already roused most of the senses.

In the opening salon, its floor covered with Moroccan rugs, one looks across through an archway to an inner hall, past a central table piled with books to where beyond, through study

OPPOSITE, CLOCKWISE FROM TOP LEFT Above the fireplace in the salon is a c.1690 portrait from Udaipur of Maharaja Jai Singh, painted on fabric; on the left is a fragment of a center medallion 17th-century Turkish Oushak rug; on the right, a Moroccan Chechaouen silk embroidery, c.1700, above an 18th-century silk embroidered bed hanging from Crete. The Georgian four-poster bed came from Harewood House in Yorkshire and is likely to be by Chippendale; the modern hangings are by Robert Kime. The front of the house, part of its Gilded Age redecoration, is the only extant facade by the late 19th-century architects the Herter Brothers; the pyramid-shaped shaped window surrounds are cut, shaped and painted pieces of metal. The bathroom sink, made in India, is a copy of a 17th-century Indian table and, like the Alhambra-inspired bathroom tilework, was commissioned by Susan. ABOVE The imposing archway frames a pair of George IV giltwood armchairs, the William De Morgan tiles behind and a view through to translucent stained-glass study doors.

doors with their original stained-glass panels, is a bedroom filled with light filtered through trees. But one doesn't look ahead for long because everywhere are objects and hangings and things to catch and hold the eye. What initially looked to me like a long multi-panelled gilded oriental screen turns out to be mounted pieces of wallpaper from the 1940s, made by Gracie, the old New York wallpaper manufacturer. "They were in a grand Park Avenue dining room and when the occupant moved to smaller quarters in her dotage she took the wallpaper with her and had it mounted on screens. I bought them at a flea market." A flea market! "Fortunately, they were an absolutely perfect fit for the space. I remember lugging them home in the back of a mini van."

Around the walls runs a cornice and frieze looking more like lace embroidery than cast plaster and bearing traces of the original gilding. (Emilio Terry, that supreme decorator, believed that "a room without a cornice is like a man without a collar" and this is grand black tie stuff – a reproduction of the same frieze is in one of the late nineteenth-century period rooms at the Met.) The long black Chinese table is piled casually with books and treasures – a nineteenth-century blue Minton dragon vase, a black and blue glass vase by Fratelli Toso, the Venetian glassblowing dynasty, a bowl by the beloved De Morgan. Tucked underneath is an Indo-Portuguese coin collector's cabinet in tortoiseshell veneer strung with ivory and dating from around the late seventeenth century but happy here in this timeless place. Over the original marble fireplace is a portrait on painted fabric of a portly Maharaja Jai Singh from Udaipur dating from around 1690. (A pendant piece to this is in the Victoria and Albert Museum.)

The bedroom on the first floor harbors a magnificent Chippendale bed bought from Harewood House in Yorkshire, where in the late eighteenth century Thomas Chippendale was given his biggest commission, to make furniture for the Lascelles family; the fabric for the hangings comes from Robert Kime.

Outside the windows is a paved courtyard with dining space bordered by an open loggia, its 12-foot-long divan bolstered and cushioned to within an inch of its arabesque life, evoking memories of a John Frederick Lewis painting and the wilder shores of love. There's a continuation of that theme in her bathroom (once the butler's pantry, as she realized when she discovered a stove behind the wall), inspired by the bath complex at the Alhambra: "I knew a shop in New York that made tiles in Fez and asked them to copy an illustration. Which they did. Perfectly. The sink made in India by Frozen-Music is a copy of a seventeenth-century Indian table that I saw in Amin Jaffer's book about Indian furniture." (Who better to provide inspiration? Dr. Jaffer is International Director of Asian Art at Christie's.)

She is witchily good at having friends, and finding people who do what she asks in decorative terms, no matter how esoteric it may be. For example, in the downstairs sitting room some beautiful calligraphy ornaments the walls. "I saw this

Silk ikat lines the glass fronts of cupboards in the sitting-room alcoves. Between is a 19th-century English cabinet covered with a jewel-like, polychrome, arabesque painted decoration. Above, copies of 16th-century Iznik plates are mounted on a silk-screened wall frieze modelled on a c.10th-century North African page from the Koran.

Koran page in a Sotheby's auction catalogue many years ago and saved the image. It's North African, probably ninth or tenth century." It was silkscreened on to tea-stained Japan paper by her friends Dan and Sue, who turn out to be the brilliant decorative painters Dan Sevigny and Sue Bachemin of SB Studios. And on the walls in the sitting room downstairs are what look like sixteenth-century Iznik plates. "I originally wanted to buy period plates. I did the math on the cost to complete the frieze and had second thoughts. So I found an artist in Istanbul who made very good copies of Iznik ware, bought a book that illustrated all of the most beautiful period Iznik plates extant, mostly in museums, and sent him pictures. He copied them with great accuracy."

The sitting room has Arts and Crafts panelling and big glass-fronted cupboards with their covetable contents, many and varied, hidden by stretched silk ikat from Uzbekistan that Susan bought in the Grand Bazaar in Istanbul. The ceiling, with its many beams, is covered in hand-screened wallpaper in an inspired combination of designs from beams in Ottoman and Middle Eastern houses and a Koran binding that she spotted in a museum collection. This ceiling tour de force is again by the Dan Sevigny and Sue Bachemin SB Studios combo, who seem to be able to turn their hand to anything. Their greatest *coup d'œil* in the house is the screen-printing on Japan paper on the walls of a small room downstairs. "It's a copy of one of the great treasures of early fourteenth-century textile art: the panels were once part of a tent made during the Mongol period, in either China or the eastern Islamic area, and used on military campaigns," Susan explains. "The original is a lampas-woven textile of silk, gilded paper, and gilded animal substrate. Some panels are now in the David Collection in Copenhagen, others in the Museum of Islamic Art in Qatar – and we have screen-printed copies right here on 16th Street in Manhattan!"

It's obsessive and it's magnificent. And magical.

ABOVE The tiles around the fireplace and the wall-mounted plates are by William De Morgan. The vase on top of the 17th-century shagreen-covered English cabinet is by Ulisse Cantagalli, as is the lusterware pot on the mantelpiece. The handsome blue pitcher is American Southern Pottery. OPPOSITE Late 19th-century Tibetan tiger rugs, which Susan collects, are laid on 19th-century Spanish floor tiles and hang on the screen-printed Japan-papered walls of the little sitting room. The Edo period Japanese hanging light is made of intricately pierced and chased bronze in a peony arabesque design.

Richard Artschwager, made from red oak, Formica, cowhide, and painted steel. (I'd advise the unwary not to try to sit on it.)

A table by Danish-American designer Jens Risom, one of the first to introduce Scandinavian design to the United States, is next to a piece by the Campana brothers – a terrifying vase that looks like a glass Medusa.

There's a kind of jubilation about the placement of art on every floor, an understanding of its aesthetic functionality. I have never been in a house with so many personally significant and historically personal pieces. It's an archive, of course, but there is nothing static or fixed about it – it breathes the energetic genius of its owner. The Diane Arbus photographs for example – she and Diane Arbus had been friends since 1958, when they met as young mothers in the Central Park "Mommy Playground," and she would often look after Diane Arbus's daughter Amy in her pram while the photographer roamed the paths looking for subjects.

She and her husband, John Jakobson, a financier, bought this house on a freezing day in 1965. "We'd looked at a lot of brownstones and then came into this and bingo we bought it in a minute."

The house has form. Elia Kazan lived here in the late 1940s, sold it to Peter Gimbels, heir to a famous department store, who made the revolutionary double-height central space and the steep staircase. Billy Baldwin, the dean of American decorators, did it up for Gimbels. "What was it like then?" I ask, sitting in the great amplitude of space that is her living/garden room, an art lover's paradise; eclectic, educative and severe all at the same time. "A garden room," she says and then in a wicked comical précis, "like a set in Auntie Mame. White-fur-coated stairs, green chintz and bamboo and wicker." (Baldwin once said, "I certainly made a lady out of wicker.") It's now cosmically removed from his version. A curving "Non-Stop" sectional sofa, the DS-600, designed in Italy in 1972 for the De Sede company and looking as long as Italy itself, sits opposite the faint typographic text WATER UNDER A BRIDGE, inscribed on the wall by sculptor Lawrence Weiner, one of the central figures in conceptual art in the 1960s, who uses language as material for construction. (If you buy a Lawrence Weiner wall installation, a team of signwriters paints it where you want it. The typeface is determined and immutable so you are buying the phrase entirely and as it is, along with the essential unique certificate

ABOVE LEFT A work by Matthew Barney above Sebastian Errazuriz's foldable *Occupy 2012* chair. ABOVE RIGHT A 1977 quadriptych portrait of Barbara by Robert Mapplethorpe hangs above a Lucite and patent leather "Corset" chair by Grosfeld House. OPPOSITE, CLOCKWISE FROM TOP A Charles Eames chair sits below a Diego Giacometti plaster mirror flanked by Italian sconces from the 1950s. *Not Picasso*, a painting by Mike Bidlo, hangs above the Salterini day bed. The table is by Gilbert Rohde. Two works by Matthew Barney flank another portrait of Barbara by Robert Mapplethorpe; *Chair*, a sculpture by Richard Artschwager, sits on the cover of *Lolita*, realized in a rug by Barbara Bloom; next to it, a side table by Jens Risom. On the mantelpiece in the Transportation Room, Poole pottery and British royal souvenirs, including an Eric Ravilious Wedgwood Coronation mug, stand in front of a 1930s poster from Heal's Mansard Gallery; to the right, a similarly iconic poster for American Airlines; on the desk, a Tizio lamp.

of authenticity.) Just below the text is a Dan Flavin fluorescent piece from 1964, and on the floor there is a table by the maverick designer and sculptor Paul Evans, "the wild card of late twentieth-century modernism," who worked mainly in metal. This sleek, high-tech table comes from his Cityscape series; another of his pieces, the Broadway chair, is in a bathroom.

She has reinvented her rooms over and over again. "I've always had an obsession with rooms and particularly rooms designed by the great women decorators — Elsie de Wolfe, Madeleine Castaing and Marie-Laure de Noailles's commissions of Jean-Michel Frank. These were some of my sources of inspiration. I guess if I have any talent at all it is in the creation of rooms, which is what I've done over and over and over." Floor after floor bears witness to that one of many talents: even the wall textures of the rooms are artful — plywood next to ribbed plaster, say — giving a feel that is different from what is being displayed.

There's also a lot of tapping into contemporary ethical movements. Although sculptor Tom Sachs apparently innocently and lightheartedly recycled those Con Edison barriers and old lumber to fashion the counters and surfaces of the installation masquerading as a tempting and well-stocked bar, he was making an intrinsic statement about the conceptual underpinnings and principles of his work, exposing how it was built, "the scars of our labor," and his system of making things out of recyclable material. (He also labelled every one of the many capitalist liquor bottles on the counter.) The bar stools are part of the artisanally inspired furniture range made by the design team BassamFellows. These modern classics are based on an old Swiss tractor seat found on the side of a road.

Another witty but serious piece, ostensibly a wood and lacquer folding chair — is an *Occupy 2012* piece by designer and artist Sebastian Errazuriz on which is painted a simple didactic question and command: HUNGRY? EAT A BANKER. In Errazuriz's work things are never quite what they seem, and his experimental style provokes thought and comedy. (Never mind cannibalism.)

Then too Frank Stella's famous apothegm "What you see is what you see" doesn't quite work here, even about his own work. For years a Frank Stella wall relief — now sold — held sway over a white wall in the big room, and each time the paint was refreshed the outline was carefully and closely painted around. What you see is a ghost of a big formidable thing — a phantasmagoric Stella.

Sold? The painting was in a sale devoted to Post-War & Contemporary Art and Design from her collection at Christie's in 2005. "The impulse . . . was to look at an empty room again, pure and simple." My mouth hangs open. A catalogue full of important stuff has gone and yet the house still has all these pieces? I love collectors. Insane.

Adam Gopnik, that brilliant essayist, once wrote: "A major divide in twentieth-century art is between those who got the fifties and couldn't get the sixties and those who got both." Barbara got both with a vengeance. Indeed, nimbly hovering over the fault line, she saw the break take place and jumped it with an unbroken stride. "I see collecting as a form of autobiography, as evidence that I lived for most of the last century and then into the new century. It's my way of staying engaged with

the world and also a way of staying engaged with myself." She still loves abstract expressionism and Frank Stella and Jasper Johns, and there's a 1966 copper tile Carl Andre piece on the floor, a Jean Prouvé chair (part of a set she once owned), Frank Gehry chairs and the singular book donkey made by Ernest Race, the English textile and furniture designer famous for his steel and molded wood chairs on which, it seemed, sat half the population of Britain during the Festival of Britain in 1951. There's more. Much more.

There are also pieces by young artists at the beginning of their careers and as they progressed: William Eggleston photographs; screen prints by Andy Warhol; a day bed by Rachel Whiteread; one of an edition of Jeff Koons's early works, *Winter Bears*, from a series of sculptures made for an exhibition, "Banality," in 1988. (Another *Winter Bears* is in the Tate Gallery.) Some see Koons as the bully in the playground, the class clown. Barbara says: "He's brilliant. Like all original artists he mines art history — they're the greatest thieves . . . if you know art history and you're a reconstructionist . . . this is a classic diptych. It's pop art and everything else and he's one of the most commanding artists to come down the pipe in the last few years."

She's always had a lot of moxie, never hesitates. "I never had any trouble making choices. Whether they were right or wrong they were my choices and that was that." She has always taken off, travelled everywhere, in pursuit of what she was interested in, and many of the pieces she bought were off the easel or out the studio within a year of their making. There is, of course, the odd maverick — a table by Edward Wormley, whose furniture represents an early convergence of historical design and modernism, sits happily near a Gio Ponti desk and magazine rack in her office, and Paul Frankl chairs hold their own with the prototype — yes the 1997 prototype — of the revolutionary knotted chair by Marcel Wanders made from lengths of hand-braided aramid and carbon fiber cord infused with epoxy resin to give it rigidity and strength. Wanders himself calls it "a little miracle." An example is in MoMA.

Looking out through the full-scale window downstairs to the white garden boundary wall you are accosted by a host of vivid enamel decorative panels. I recognized them, with nostalgia, as having been on the facade of Alexander's department store opposite Bloomingdale's decades ago. These disregarded shopfront pieces turn out to be archetypal examples of the work of Stefan Knapp, a Polish painter and sculptor who worked in England and developed and patented a technique of enamel paint on steel. Barbara, being Barbara, rescued them when the building was demolished. Never a better example of her belief that "if you're a highly visual person you interpret the world by looking at it, or looking at its artifacts."

In 1979 she was dazzled by *Stilnovo*, a book by the architectural historian Christian Borngräber about the imagination and fantasy of furniture and general design in the fifties. He became a close friend and under his influence she started collecting singular and important fifties furniture and industrial design objects. "Though I love all furniture I decided early on I had to live in my own time. And that is what collecting allows one to do — if you acquire things that relate to your own life, you have a much more significant attachment to them. What made me

Barbara's Grosfeld House Lucite bed and bedside table.

want to buy this furniture was its biomorphism. In a way it's like surrealism on legs. Suddenly those liquid fluid furniture forms were so appealing to me like Dalí's melting watches I'd seen at the Modern so long ago, and I think they're still appealing."

Examples abound of the interlocking and omnivorous worlds of design, fashion art and furniture. She hunted down the chairs made in brass and resin flex that Carlo Mollino designed in 1958 as a wedding present for Gio Ponti's daughter Lisa. Only six chairs were made as part of a suite. The eyes of different beholders read this chair differently. For some it is brazenly erotic, other see a cloven hoof back attesting to his fascination with the occult. Barbara's Lucite and patent leather "Corset" chair, made by the New York company Grosfeld House (pioneers throughout the 1930s and 1940s in the use of Lucite for furniture – which I fear are called Glassics), seems almost the precursor of the Mollino piece. In her bedroom are more Lucite pieces from Grosfeld House, including the glamorous headboard and beside tables.

On every floor there are pieces freighted with history. Take, for example, the "Mexican Bookshelf," designed by the French architect and designer Charlotte Perriand in 1953 for the Maison du Mexique at Cité Internationale Universitaire de Paris. This is often attributed to Jean Prouvé (it was produced by Atelier Prouvé), and his name attracted higher bids at auction. It is only quite recently that Perriand's fundamental importance as the author of great pieces has been fully recognized.

"Everything I acquire somehow relates to a memory of my own life. If I get it, if I buy it, if it becomes a part of my life, it's because somehow it's tipped off some unconscious sensation, and I know that a lot of people who relate deeply to art have this sensation. It's not unique to me, it's described by others."

She carries a swathe of knowledge of modern art and design in her head. It is her real subject, and everything she does in her life's work is both a critique and homage to the true thing.

So when you walk though this house and through its rooms you're not just walking through rooms or even a retrospective look at a life. You're walking through a continuing, felt, intense, immediate, direct, vivid autobiography; autobiography mingled with memoir and with unwritten chapters in waiting, waiting for her next swoops. The medium in which it is written is her life, the consequence of a profound, relentless, unquenchable need. "If you said to me, what do you want more than anything I'd say – Surprise me. I want to be surprised by the future and I hope I am."

ABOVE The focus of Barbara's bedroom is an enormous photograph of a room in Carlo Mollino's hidden apartment in Turin. In front of it, a Regency sofa and a Grosfeld House chair. OPPOSITE In the bathroom are two Warhol screenprints: *Nixon*, which is part of a large edition made in support of the McGovern campaign; and *Liz*, signed and dated 1965.

TIME'S FINE TELESCOPE

AMY FINE COLLINS

Amy Fine Collins's apartment is such fun, so imperiously, light-heartedly purple and with such a lapidary jewel-like quality that it's hard to find prose to match; underneath its style and individuality are parody, intelligence, fantasy and humor. Much like its owner. It's also wittily referential and by way of being a homage to the cosmetics entrepreneur Helena Rubinstein. You can't quite read the apartment – though you could still get a frisson of delight from looking at it – unless you know something of the inspirational drive of the two amazing women behind it, Helena then, Amy now.

Amy's garnering of furniture and paintings from various sales of Helena Rubinstein's possessions shows the cosmetics queen to be have been a discerning, acute and vain collector, with a great eye for both contemporary art and self-promotion. "For a start she was so avant-garde," Amy says. Helena Rubinstein had distinct ideas about how her apartments should look and that look became a sort of benchmark for the baroque culture-of-excess decoration of the times: satin padded walls, silvered grotto furniture, blackamoors – of course – and elaborate French salon furniture of the mid-nineteenth century. She had a large collection of pictures by Picasso, Matisse and neo-romantic and surrealist painters and many – many! – portraits of herself commissioned from, among others, Salvador Dalí, Pavel Tchelitchew and Paul César Helleu. There are at least eight big portraits of her throughout Amy's apartment.

Amy Fine Collins's official title is Special Correspondent to *Vanity Fair*, which is a catch-all title for being at the center of things in a certain world. She has a long reach. She is an art historian and a writer, a muse for many fashion designers (most particularly for Geoffrey Beene) and a focus for style mavens; and her pieces for Vanity Fair encompass a good deal more than fashion and style – her article on the sex trafficking of young Americans, "The Girls Next Door," was not only the most-read article in the history of vanityfair.com at the time, it helped change the law of the United States. She speaks very fast, makes one laugh, and doesn't mince her words.

OPPOSITE In the sitting room is a 1930s Lucite chair by Ladislas Medgyes, one of the first ever made, etched with a rose, from the estate of Helena Rubinstein; behind it is a 1929 red chalk and watercolor portrait of Helena Rubinstein, by M.L. Closset. Above is an abstract still life by Amy's mother, Elsa Honig Fine. Tucked in the corner is one of a pair of Tapa barkcloth-covered screens built by the photographer Horst. On the glass coffee table is a multi-layered glass collage chessboard by sculptor Dustin Yellin. PAGES 186–187 Light pours into the sitting room through south-facing windows. Between them is one of three exquisite Baguès sconces, similar to those in Cole Porter's Waldorf Astoria apartment. The 1930s Venetian mirror above the fireplace came from the estate of Helena Rubinstein and the 1950s fire screen below is by Federico Pallavicini, who designed packaging and decorated salons and houses for her. The c.1970 rug was designed by Emilio Pucci.

ABOVE In the dining room, light-hearted panels by Marcel Vertès hang on walls painted by Robert Hoven. The pickled and white-painted Italian chairs are by Syrie Maugham, next to Nicaraguan designer Mario Villa's metal palm-frond chairs covered in Gene Meyer scarves. A plaster sculpture of Mae West by Gladys Lewis stands between bronze urns by Tiffany & Co., of c.1890. OPPOSITE The hallway carpet, custom-made by Gene Meyer, leads the eye to a pair of Victorian folding screens framing the dining room doorway. Two palm torchères flank a console and looking glass, all designed by Serge Roche; the pink opaline glass vases are from the estate of Helena Rubinstein. The set of silver-gilt grotto chairs – two here, others in the living room – is probably Venetian.

Geoffrey Beene was a huge influence in her life and style (in a witty triple entendre he called her Amuse). She met him after he read her article "The Wearable Rightness of Beene," in which, as an art historian, she analyzed the aesthetic decisions and finished work of this greatest of American fashion designers, and he wrote: "How is it possible that you know me better than I know myself . . . when we haven't even met?" He influenced her immaculate look – "The look I maintain today still bears Beene's defining imprint."

Before I met her, though she was a Presence, an arbiter of style in the world of Hautezine, I thought that one of the key phrases defining Amy Fine Collins was the title of a book she co-authored, *Simple Isn't Easy*, subtitled *How to Find Your Personal Style and Look Fantastic Every Day!* (Which she does.) And thus I imagined that her apartment just off Park Avenue would have the simplicity of, say, a haiku.

Fâcheuse illusion. The place where this long-legged, raven-haired person lives, with her husband, Professor Bradley Collins, and beautiful daughter, Flora, and VIP cat, Leo, has a distinct aesthetic. This is neo-baroque par excellence. Curious, hybrid, highly strung, fancy and fanciable, grand and enchanting, it brims with éclat – as well as with key pieces from Helena Rubinstein's legacy tracked down from auctions over the years. The screen in front of the original fireplace in her sitting room was painted by Federico Pallavicini, who in the late fifties was an artistic consultant and interior designer for Madame, as she liked to be called. (Earlier he had helped create the innovative magazine *Flair* for Fleur Cowles.) Above the mantelpiece is a mirror left to Helena Rubinstein's nephew Oscar, sold at auction after his death.

The Collins apartment is not pastiche, but it is – as Helena Rubinstein's was – a reaction to mainstream interior design. It manifests itself in Amy's exuberant love of shapes and detail and the decorative possibilities of ornament, exemplified in her own personal way of dressing: a ferocity of elegance.

Many signifiers from the fifties are at home here – paintings by Marcel Vertès, the French-Hungarian costume designer and illustrator who won two Academy Awards for his work on the 1952 film *Moulin Rouge*, and whose fifties murals in the Café Carlyle are much loved by New Yorkers; drawings by the cherished artist, illustrator and designer Christian Bérard – Bébé to his friends – and pieces by contemporary artists, usually friends.

Then there's the Léger painting found by her husband in the south of France when he was thirteen (precocious or what?). Every day she writes – and she writes a lot – at a desk once owned by Hugh Hefner. (The dealer wasn't sure whether he should tell her of its provenance or not. As if she cared.) A note from her daughter, Flora – "You are the beest Moma in

the wole world" — is pinned near to a Skrebneski drawing and to sketches of Amy as a child by her formidably gifted mother, Elsa Honig Fine. "I worked on that," Amy says, "I could get her attention if I posed for her." Her mother is a much-awarded writer, art historian and professor, the author of a pioneering study, *The Afro-American Artist: A Search for Identity*, published in 1973; her father, Harold Fine, was a psychologist and psycho-analyst. "I also loved art but, although I was a good artist as a child, I stopped. I thought, I am never going to be good enough as a painter so I completely converted that aesthetic drive into clothing." Indeed. She once said, "I will be my own canvas."

And if it is hard to put into words the visual lightning that is her living space, it's even more of a conundrum to describe her as she moves through it like a vixen. Moves? No! Glides? No! Strides? Drifts? No! Glissades? Put them all together and you get this lanky, fascinating creature's manner of movement. She looks as though she has been created by a team of alien artists who have been sent fashion drawings by Joe Eula or Antonio Lopez and who think that is what the human female looks like. She would never do as a template. She has said herself that she makes a self-portrait every day.

But I'm running ahead of myself, as one is wont to do in her company. The long ravishing hall stretches the length of the apartment, creating an enfilade on either side — an idea from vatic interior designer and architect Robert Couturier which changed the whole axis of the apartment. (He once said, disarmingly, "I'm completely addicted to luxury. I have no ability for anything else.") He found the hanging lamps in Paris. The walls are painted by Robert Hoven, the Catskill-based decorator and (this is much in keeping with the high-spirited ethos of the thing) former opera singer. Indeed, he has painted almost every room in this apartment, with impeccable style and unwavering line.

Two plaster palm torchères by Serge Roche flank his console table and overmirror (while underneath hides a loony portrait of Ophelia by Vertès). Everything done by Serge Roche was chic; the son of an antique dealer, he carried on dealing, especially in old Venetian looking glasses, and then used the crafty old mirror-makers' techniques to create his own spin, which he called the Panache style. He was fascinated by frames, by mirrors, by nature's miracles of shape and form, especially shells, coral and rocks; and many of his lovely objects and decorative pieces — furniture, vases obelisks — are made of mirrored elements mixed with Venetian glass beads. The multi-layered glass collage chessboard by sculptor Dustin Yellin on a table in the sitting room, playing just this side of kitsch (as so much neo-baroque does), has faint if unconscious echoes of his work.

ABOVE LEFT Beyond the leopard-print-covered three-lobed ottoman in the living room are portraits by Dorothy Gillespie of fashion historian Richard Martin and Amy's mother, Elsa Honig Fine; a metal maquette, also by Gillespie, hangs on the cabinet between them. On it, a bronze bust of actress Linda Christian by Jacques Lipchitz stands in front of a gouache of Barbara Hutton by fashion illustrator Carl Erickson (Eric). To the right, a Christian Bérard fashion drawing hangs above a profile portrait of Helena Rubinstein by the Polish painter and engraver Louis Marcoussis. ABOVE RIGHT A digital portrait of Amy by Iké Udé above a Directoire-style day bed covered in Manuel Canovas cut velvet. The hallway walls are painted by Robert Hoven.

The three-dimensional palms are echoed in the ghostly *trompe l'œil* wall decorations – again by Hoven – and on the original parquet floor a long tufted rug called "Multiscreen," designed by Gene Meyer and made of rectangular squares in rainbow colors, pulls the hall into an exercise in perspective.

A big portrait of Amy – a manipulated image digitally rendered by Iké Udé, a Nigerian-American journalist turned artist who works in New York and in Nollywood, the Nigerian film industry ("he sought me out to be in his magazine *aRude*") – hangs over a day bed she found in a Christian Louboutin shop which was closing down. She re-covered it in an exuberant Canovas fabric. She often pounces on small old fancy boutiques with unusual fittings which are on the way out. That's also how she came across the pair of Billy Baldwinesque gilt bamboo and glass side tables in Hélène Arpels's shoe boutique on Park Avenue. (Even these are layered in fashion history – Hélène Arpels was part of the Van Cleef and Arpels dynasty and the Manolo Blahnik of her day.) In the hall is a pair from the set of six ravishing and gilded grotto chairs – probably Venetian – which Amy bought from a Thai dealer in New York.

In the purple-tinged dining room the Venetian sconces with their tumble of glass balls and prisms come from a Gloria Vanderbilt sale and the walls are painted by Robert Hoven with subtle pink, silver, lilac and green stripes of varying widths. One of the most remarkable pieces is a low delirious *verre églomisé* cabinet signed "Franky 1936." Matelots, windswept maidens, shells and patterns in rich purples, reds and yellows frolic across its doors. Unknown artist? French? Enchanting in any case and from the Helena Rubinstein estate. The chairs are covered in scarves designed by Gene Meyer. On the dining room sideboard stands a voluptuous plaster figure of Mae West by Gladys Lewis Bush – the hour-glass torso was used in a radical design by Schiaparelli for her scent "Shocking" and came from a sale held by Schiaparelli's granddaughter, model Marisa Berenson. The advertisements for Schiaparelli's scents were all drawn by Marcel Vertès (everywhere you turn in this apartment you are in a lexicon of mid-twentieth-century fashion). An archway leads through to a small breakfast room hung with slinky fashion drawings including a Kenneth Paul Block drawing of three departed doyennes of fashion, Babe Paley, C.Z. Guest and Diana Vreeland, wearing the same Balenciaga evening coat.

The other end of the hall leads towards a prettily proportioned sitting room, with two fine twelve-paned windows. There's an air of fantasy here, a layout that is fresh though laden with memories and resonance. In the middle of the room sits a triangular deep-buttoned ottoman rescued from a junk shop and restored with meticulous, not to say obsessive, care. It is covered in leopard-skin fabric, with a deep passementerie trim, and its finial is a rose quartz sphere perched on a specially cast tiny silver-plated twig.

The cascading glass Baguès sconces were found in New York, at Malmaison, the shop owned by Roger Prigent, antiquaire and dealer whose simple maxim, underlying his catholicity of taste, was that "everything is chic or not chic."

On either side of a cabinet are rather Grant Woodish-Gothic portraits by Dorothy Gillespie of Amy's mother, Elsa Honig Fine, and of Richard Martin, a leading art and fashion scholar.

(At the time of his death in 1999 he was curator of the Costume Institute at the Metropolitan Museum of Art.) On its handle hangs a little abstract metal maquette also by Dorothy Gillespie and hanging above is a portrait of Barbara Hutton by fashion illustrator and painter Carl Erickson (Eric). Leaning out in a marked manner is a bust of the actress Linda Christian by Jacques Lipchitz. Even on the floor you are walking over a palimpsest of dense fashion and social history – Emilio Pucci, that grand fashion designer of the fifties, and René Crevel, sad surrealist poet and artist, designed the rare and sophisticated rugs.

A pair of screens, folded and tucked unobtrusively near the windows, was owned by the photographer Horst P. Horst, who adored Amy. After his death his adopted son, Ricky Horst, said, "Horst would want you to have a few things." Amy still has the signed note written in capital letters, "HOLD THE SCREEN AND THE BOOKCASE FOR AMY FINE COLLINS. R. HORST." The bookcase by Jean-Michel Frank, made of straw and wood, is in the main bedroom. (Billy Baldwin described Frank as "the last genius of French furniture.") The fabric on the screens originally belonged to Coco Chanel. Horst had taken the famous photograph of Chanel reclining on a satin-covered sofa and she never looked more alluring. Amy traces the story. "Chanel developed a crush on Horst and as a thank you she sent him a lot of stuff and among it was a length of rare and valuable barkcloth. Of course he couldn't leave well alone and stuck the cloth on to a Bauhaus screen and the glue he used has damaged the bark irreparably. The Met would like to have used them for an exhibition but they are too fragile to be moved."

Many of Amy's delicious things come from secret sources. Secret in two senses: where she found them, and she sometimes keeps them secret for a while before inserting them into the apartment. She regrets the plums that got away. Her Lucite chairs are by Ladislas Medgyes, a pioneering Hungarian artist who used all kinds of revolutionary new materials to design the packaging for some of Helena Rubinstein's best-selling perfumes. "They are part of a set," says Amy. "He designed her Lucite bed which Billy Wilder bought from her estate and I bought these chairs at Christie's years later." Her voice is maybe a little bit sad when she speaks of the bed. "I didn't buy it because I was worried about overspending and then where would I place it?" The subtext is that of many wives whose husbands are not collectors. (I know the subtext too well.)

"I cyclically get uncontrollable urges to bid at an auction – and win. I'm a bit of a bottom fisher," she says, of the way she often finds forgotten things at the end of a sale, like the pretty flower painting in her sitting room which she found at Christie's. It was by "a couturier who had stopped being a couturier." Molyneux. "No one else seemed to know who he was. I shop in shops and in flea markets, especially the Paris flea markets. Without which my apartment would not be adequately furnished."

The word adequate is not one that fits here. Dazzling is better. A nineteenth-century aesthete and art critic (and perhaps multiple murderer), one Thomas Griffiths Wainewright, who had a passionate love for stuff (stuff in the Shakespearean sense – "We are such stuff as dreams are made on"), once wrote: "Things that spring up under my nose dazzle me. I must look at them through Time's Telescope." That's it here.

THINGS BEING VARIOUS

JEAN PAGLIUSO & TOM COHEN

At first prowl the apartment belonging to artist Jean Pagliuso and her husband, Tom Cohen, seems sedate enough – which impression is right out of sync given her occupation, her imagination and the wide, not to say wild-eyed, look with which she views the world – not just with those eyes but through the lens of her camera, the tool of her art. Seems sedate. And is comfortable. But take a closer look and you see, arranged apparently randomly on shelves and surfaces, an eclectic massing of found and inherited objects, pieces from friends, things collected from her travels. There is no hint of the extravaganza that marks some collectors, or the *omnium gatherum* of others, and you register that these ensembles are an anthology of talismanic images and instructions. "World is crazier and more of it than we think, Incorrigibly plural." Jean might have said it if Louis MacNeice hadn't already.

Here is a skull of a ram with its great curved antlers, straight out of Georgia O'Keeffe, looming above a Mexican doll of the dead; a group of pebbles ("We're rock crazy - collect them from every beach!") making counterpoint to ancient Anasazi pottery and ceramics by Elisabeth Kley; a copy of *Peter Beard: Fifty Years of Portraits*, with every page annotated and personalized for her, next to a Campbell soup can signed by Andy Warhol, a gift from Anna Wintour to mark the birth of their daughter, Jesse. It later exploded. (It becomes apparent as one walks though the apartment that Jesse, now grown-up, is a fine artist.)

Wander on, over the Berber, Navajo and Tuareg reed and leather-strung rugs, through the open flow of the rooms, past walls (artful in themselves) laden with more images. A photograph of a mud mosque in Mali, a shutter from an Indonesian house, a Franco Clemente watercolor, a Caio Fonseca painting, and a portrait of St Catherine by a follower of Bronzino.

Here too are Moroccan bowls (there's a tale to tell), Shino glazed stoneware, a Robert Graham sculpture, a Mies van der Rohe chair, a bronze sculpture by Ahn Duong of her foot in a high-heeled shoe, Chinese axes from the Qijia culture, a Liangzhu jade disc – oh, a host of things, evidence of what Susan Sontag called the "insatiability of the photographing eye."

Jean Pagliuso is a photographer. Well, that's putting it mildly. Born and raised in California, she worked for *Mademoiselle* in New York before becoming a photographer, mostly in fashion, for every notable magazine one could think of, and in the film industry too – she did posters for movies including *American Gigolo* and *Thieves Like Us*.

Then in the mid-1990s ("nothing of [her] . . . but doth suffer a sea-change/Into something rich and strange"), she began to experiment with a different grammar, different printing processes, a different ethic. She travelled widely – Cambodia, India, New Mexico, Peru and Turkey – photographing endangered places of ritual and environment. (She also dealt nimbly with that old dilemma of mother/working woman. When Jesse was very young she decided to close her studio and become a full-time mother. The experiment lasted seven months – "I found that most of the time was spent doing the housework and shopping that I do anyway, I just spent a lot longer doing it. So I went back to work.")

She mostly works with a Hasselblad camera. She has a hands-on approach to her printing and uses every kind of antique and modern process, including photogravure, with meticulous exactitude, to make her art. She's been inspired by old temple rubbings and prints images using a hand-applied silver gelatin emulsion brushed on handmade Japanese rice paper; or she might use thin sheets of handmade Thai paper brushed with silver emulsion on to which a negative is exposed in the darkroom, giving a seductive texture to the finished image. Many beautiful examples are here in these rooms.

The photographs I most love are her portrait series of hens and roosters, who by their very nature look insane. Her series *The Poultry Suite* is described as strictly formalized and, indeed, the prints are the same size, format and finish, but there is nothing else formal about the ravishing and sometimes comical black and white accounts of these exotic creatures that we so take for granted. She strips them of all familiarity. They look only this side of lunacy, peering out at the viewer or in proud profile, hair puffed out or standing on end like fowlish Struwwelpeters. Every image marks each hen as a total individual and one that you wouldn't necessarily want to meet on a dark night; and, as one who kept fancy hens for years, I know whereof I speak. (Jean refers to a painting given to her by Susan Sarandon as a "happily little morbid chicken.")

This duplex sits high above a vastly busy stretch of midtown Fifth Avenue - you can see the Flatiron Building from one side and One World Trade Center on the other. But it's quiet up here. The great *coup de théâtre* is the light tumbling down a pale wood staircase from new windows high above. Until a few years ago this staircase and floor did not exist – there was just a flat roof. Then her husband, who had presciently obtained those most desirable of top-floor things called roof or air lights, "went ahead with breaking up through the ceiling to a new top floor, making another new set of rooms upstairs." There was enough space to have a handsome garden which included – joy of joys – the existing water tower. (These urban icons of New York stoutly rise all over Manhattan, primordial, ubiquitous, old-fashioned, defying technology, built as they are of Canadian cedar held together with galvanized steel bands. The barrels can hold ten thousand gallons of water, last for decades, and there are around fifteen thousand in the city; the artist Rachel Whiteread even cast one in shimmering resin for her first New York installation.)

A cardboard sculpture by Oto Gilen, used as a fruit bowl, rests on a striking curly maple dining table with inlays of purpleheart wood (amaranth) and mahogany designed by M. Nord Haggerty. In the kitchen (through the mahogany room divider), a work by Cy Twombly stands on a high shelf near to *Hydrangeas*, a photograph by Alessandra Sanguinetti.

ABOVE Propped up against the staircase wall's beautiful plaster finish are photographs by Ralph Gibson. OPPOSITE ABOVE On the wall between the bookshelves is a Cubist painting, probably by Georges Valmier; propped against the wall is a painting of pecking chickens given to Jean by Susan Sarandon. OPPOSITE BELOW An array of photographs from Jean's *Poultry Suite* dominates the kitchen. To the right of the tap, resting against the hand-painted American tiles, is a Kallitype salted print of pears by Jean.

To make such a radical change and insert a staircase and a new wall into an existing space took a lot of thinking about, and the solutions are chaste and visually elegant. The apartment is an amalgam of styles, representing thirty years of architectural and personal transformation. Beginning with an open loft layout, it evolved into a duplex apartment. Three distinct stages led to the current look: Nord Haggerty designed the first, and everything was leather, chrome and handsome wood window trim. The second was a complete redo by William McDonough, sometimes called "the green architect" and co-author of the book *Cradle to Cradle: Remaking the Way We Make Things* — so not a surprising choice, given the conservation ethos evident everywhere here. He did the roof and the roof deck and was responsible for finding Steve Balser, the fine plasterer.

The third stage was a partial renovation with Lee Skolnick, who designed the stairs; his aim is "to generate a fully integrated architectural experience to transcend a space's purpose," and this staircase is both a functional object and a sharp sculpture.

The putty-colored wall is a major feature in the house, soaring high and linking the rooms. "We were trying to transition from one room to other as smoothly as possible," Jean says, and the surfaces have been brought to a fine diamond-trowelled plaster finish by Steve Balser, proselytizer for traditional lime putty plaster. The materials he uses are mixtures of slaked lime, fine sands, pulverized marble and quartz, powdered earth pigments, metallic oxides, gypsum and water . . . totally traditional and with a result as smooth as a baby's bum.

There are few doors in the apartment — a Woodhenge-y mahogany room divider which doubles as a pantry divides the kitchen from the dining room and was conceived by Lee Skolnick's architectural firm, LHSA. The striking curly maple dining table, with its inlays of purpleheart wood and mahogany, was designed by Nord Haggerty and made by Billy Russell, a joiner who had his studio just doors away. Jean bought the butcher's block and the lovely old deal table in the kitchen from Balassus, a much-loved but now defunct antique shop in Amagansett. (Some of the chairs in the sitting room came from a downtown shop, Cobweb, also now gone; one of the things I heard over and over again from collectors was the lament of how the old antique shops and markets where you could make felicitous discoveries have disappeared in New York, driven out by colossal rental price rises.)

On the table nearby are those big North African dishes. Jean and Tom found and reserved them in a Moroccan market; but when they came back to collect them they found that a detaining order had been slapped on them to keep them in the country. Long story short — "They were released and we schlepped them home." Since Jean could charm birds of the trees it's understandable. I spy a photograph of the actor and musical star Nell Campbell, of *The Rocky Horror Show* and the best legs in the world, taken years ago, and later I ask Nell about Jean. "She does everything with style, her clothes, her home and of course her

The fireplace in the living room is by William McDonough and on it rest two encaustic tiles by Sheila Berger, a case of teeth, and an Egyptian head of a young woman. Above is a 16th-century Italian painting of St Catherine. The leather chairs were found in an antique shop in downtown Manhattan. On the right, propped on the skirting board, a portrait of Jean by her daughter, Jesse; above, an elephant photograph by Peter Beard.

photographs. After holidays with friends she would make them exquisite little photo albums, perhaps ten photos from their trip, usually landscapes, developed in faded sepia or pale black and white, printed on thick, rough-edged, handmade paper bound in string or some such. She would sometimes paste tiny curiosities on to the photos or hand-tint them. They were much coveted."

There's a remarkable Cubist painting signed G. Valmier hanging on the bookcase wall. They inherited it and it got a new lease of life when it arrived. "We love it," Jean says.

In this remarkable, discreet, streetwise apartment you're not only in the lair of a forager of the fleeting, you're in an exemplar of the cross-cultural life of a circle of artists living in New York now and of someone who never takes the act of seeing for granted. I asked her to describe it. "A mix of crazy things. That's all."

CLOCKWISE FROM TOP LEFT On the wall, a graphite moon drawing by Juliet Jacobson; nestled together propped on the floor, two images of a nude by Irving Penn – Jean bought one, Tom the other. The tall inscribed wooden piece is an Indonesian reading aid for children; Jean found the figure of a man displaying necklaces in a jewellery shop in Mali; and the ceramic bowl inlaid with ivory and silver was bought in the medina in Marrakech. The tall dark figure is a Santo from Santa Fe; on the right, a decorated Anasazi bowl with a kill hole (this was part of an Anasazi burial rite: the bowl was "killed" by piercing a hole in the bottom, and it was then placed over the head of the dead body, allowing the spirit to escape). The pot on the lower shelf is also Anasazi and next to it is Campbell's soup can signed by Andy Warhol, a gift from Anna Wintour for the birth of daughter Jesse.

ABOVE The water tower in the roof garden glows as the sun sets.

WELL FASHIONED

TIMOTHY VAN DAM & RONALD WAGNER

So here we are in Venice in 1499 in *The Dream of Poliphilus*. Oh, no, we're not. We're in New York City's Harlem, near Convent Avenue, in a neighborhood of tree-lined streets and well-kept buildings. But all the same, in my flight of fancy, we could be in Venice in the olden dream days, rather than inside this Harlem brownstone townhouse.

The Dream of Poliphilus, as above, is a mysterious allegory in which Poliphilus dreams he is moving with much sensuous spirit through a house. "And about the sides of the walles, there were placed Settles, of color betwixt a yealow and tawny, passing well turned and fashioned, covered over with green Velvet and bowlstered with soem soft stuffe or feather easie to sit up, attached with nayles of Golde." Well, I'm not sure about the gold nails, but the rest fits the house like a dream. Especially the yealows and tawnys.

So who is the genius of the house? Well, two: Ronald Wagner and Timothy Van Dam, who have been partners both in life and in their interior design business for over thirty years. They live in the now-fashionable Hamilton Heights Historic District, which takes its name from Alexander Hamilton, one of the Founding Fathers of the United States, who had a fine house known as the Grange on his estate here – then many miles away from midtown Manhattan.

There is block after block here of elegant late nineteenth- and early twentieth-century row houses in wildly varying styles — architects seemed to have fun then in a way they don't now, and they lathered turrets, gothicky windows, gargoyles, oriel windows and crenellations on to versions of the Beaux Arts, Queen Anne, Romanesque Revival, French Gothic and Flemish Renaissance styles. The notable architect Clarence True, who built this house, is credited with transforming the look of the townhouse on the Upper West Side. His radical innovation: instead of a high stoop, and a climb of ten or twelve steps, his entrances were only two or three steps up.

They moved here from their one-room flat near Gramercy Park in 1985, a time when buying this far north of Central Park was regarded as experimental pioneering. The minute they came here they loved it. "We had already looked in Brooklyn, the Lower East Side, the Village – we were too late, or we couldn't afford it, or it was too far away – and then we came up to explore this neighborhood and our jaws just dropped. Basically, we fell in love with the architecture and then with the house, its height and scale."

So, a bit more history. Ronald Wagner and Timothy Van Dam would seem to have been separated at birth. They both graduated from Pratt Institute, both later taught there, Wagner/Van Dam Design and Decoration was founded in 1993, when they joined their individual practices. Their workplace, the engine room of their business, is completely different from the rest of the house.

Mementoes from the couple's travels fill their Gothic Revival Orientalist Library, from top (small lanterns from Patmos hanging from the ceiling's Moorish star plasterwork) to bottom (the zebra skin from South Africa). On top of the mantel, in front of a pink pygmy feather headdress, a statue of *Romulus and Remus and the Capitoline Wolf* is a reminder of their visits to Rome.

Carved out of the former attic, reached by a narrow staircase, it looks like the inside of a swish super-yacht, with its pale oak wood, board and bead panelling and sleek lines, its meticulously filed fabric swatches and sample books on the office shelves, and plans for ongoing projects on the desks.

They wanted their house to regain its lost *grande dame* beauty, and have assiduously collected pieces of the period. It's filled with objects, but it's not cluttered. Space is as important as the thing itself, especially when it comes to hanging pictures or placing furniture, and the use of interior space changes at every era. Wagner and Van Dam are very aware of this.

In certain rooms, far from being in Venice, one could be in late Victorian times, given Ron and Timothy's untroubled mingling of the American Empire, Aesthetic movement and American Gothic Revival objects and furniture with whatever else takes their fancy. In the Orientalist Library four votive lights, found in Patmos, orbit like little moons around the gilt bronze Gothic Revival chandelier. A Moorish plasterwork star built into the ceiling gleams above an ebonized American sofa and two side chairs upholstered in tent-striped fabric and passementerie. A surprising zebra skin lies on the floor and four large ebonized bookcases face up to an American Empire table crowded with obelisks, candlesticks and a model of that saddest of sculptures, *The Dying Gaul.*

Upstairs, in the Chinese Room, a stuffed egret supervises the Victorian taxidermy bell jar in the middle of a Reform Gothic table. An Aesthetic movement cabinet is filled with transferware of the same period. The carpet is 1920s Chinese Deco, with a lurid color scheme of lavender, purple and green, and the same colors were courageously used as the basis for the room's decoration. A painting after Alma-Tadema, found in the much-mourned 26th Street flea market, was fitted into a Wagner family frame, and now hangs above the display cabinets.

There is steady attention to detail, and artful retrieval. They found old lace panels that were so dirty and in such bad shape that they seemed beyond repair, but Timothy took them up to their country house in Taghkanic in New York State where he assembled a 12-foot garden table and a gigantic pan filled with water. He soaked the panels flat, soaped, rinsed, soaped, rinsed, and starched them with cooked starch. And then painstakingly restored them. The more you look the more you see the workmanship behind the restoration here. They are also good at finding things — among them a huge pier mirror of mercury glass, retrieved from a dumpster, an American Empire center

OPPOSITE On the spacious stair landing is the family piano; on top, a contemporary nude lounges alongside classical figures and a Swedish birdcage. On the walls are black and white silk screens by Edwina Sandys. A William Morris paper, "Pomegranate," edges the ceiling. ABOVE A chandelier bought at a Harlem thrift shop presides over the dining room, which also houses a back-to-back double portrait of the two owners, painted by John Woodrow Kelley, Wagner's college roommate.

table, covered in layers of green paint with original water gilt cornucopia beneath, and a parlor settee and chairs which Ron spotted as by the nineteenth-century firm Pottier & Stymus.

The city of Buffalo, Ron's hometown, seems to be a special treasure trove. "It has a rich past." Ron says. "When the Erie Canal was built it entered a golden, glorious time. People had huge houses filled with good furniture, and so antique shops had treasures. It's having a rebirth now." Among the things from there is a sideboard bought for $90, a pair of Corinthian columns found by Ron's father in a trash bin, the Chinese temple lantern in the guest bathroom, and a drop-front desk with remarkable strapwork by Kimbel and Cabus, a nineteenth-century New York company noted for its Modern Gothic and Anglo-Japanese style furniture.

On the way up the panelled staircase, through the original Italianate arcade, I goggle at a depiction of a handsome and muscular Zeus lost in thought, a bit after Flandrin, and then realize it's a portrait of Ron. There's also a back-to-back portrait of the two of them, in the dining room. John Woodrow Kelley, who was at Pratt with Ron, painted both of these.

Across the stair hall is the living room, the light from huge windows filtered through lace panels onto an ebonized cabinet Ron spotted in a junk shop in Tucson, Arizona, and the restored center table from the flea market. The room is warmed on chilly evenings by the original porcelain gas fireplace logs, high-tech circa 1895. "When we have a party it looks marvellous."

They're not shy about color, these two. The dining room has warm Pompeian red walls with a yellow cornice and dado, and snowy table linen throws up a sheen of light towards a glass-clustered chandelier found in Sister Pugh's Harlem thrift store. Nineteenth-century Grand Tour souvenirs stand on the mantelshelf, the whole effect a mosaic of a bourgeois room where Washington Irving might have dined.

"Each period of history has its own way of seeing things — its own 'period eye,' as it were," wrote Peter Thornton in *Authentic Décor: The Domestic Interior 1620–1920*. And, lo and behold, here fastened in place is the most authentic, the archetypal Victorian detail — the needlepoint and beaded fireplace mantel lambrequin in the library. Perfect period eyes.

ABOVE The main bathroom has the original plain white tiles with their shell and ribbon topping. A bust of Apollo (sporting a coral necklace from Ron's mother) greets those who enter. Vintage finds include a recently discovered fireplace, an old gas light fixture and a mirror over the tub. OPPOSITE In the library, a Japanese *obi* is draped across a Gothic Reform table. A collection of brown and white transferware china anchors a giant cabinet bought in Buffalo. Above it is a reproduction of a Lawrence Alma-Tadema work in a frame supplied by Ron's grandparents.

FANTASY IN HARLEM

JAMES FENTON & DARRYL PINCKNEY

You could devote a whole book to James Fenton and Darryl Pinckney's house, in Mount Morris Park in Harlem, an amazing fantasy palace which you mightn't be surprised to find in Dickensian London but don't expect to come across on the upper reaches of Manhattan.

Once through the impressive and imposing pillared portico with its carved lintels and arch, through a bluebeard-looking front door ("the letter box was a hole cut into the mahogany"), you're in the first reception hall, aka down the rabbit hole in a house that is 25 feet wide and 10,000 square feet. "It is big," James allows, "and I love it. When I first saw the front entrance I thought it might be by McKim, Mead & White, as it's very much in that style, but the architect was Frank Hill Smith, a Bostonian artist, architect and interior designer who obviously paid great attention to what Stanford White and his colleagues were up to, as this entrance is a version of what they had done a year before, at the Judson Church on Washington Square."

Once through the door you're in a cosmos full of remarkable color, entrancing objects, and enticing spaces which include oval rooms, snaking staircases, inviting landings (rooms in themselves), which in turn reveal stained-glass windows, panelled walls, color heaped on vibrato color, textures of many colors and provenances, textiles from all over the world — heaped velvets and hanging linens — intriguing paintings, elaborate plaster-work and collected treasures, archaeological finds, German Expressionist prints, daguerreotypes, American furniture (Emeco Navy chairs), English furniture, rarities, and various relics, terracotta tiles, sculpture — all contained without pretension or studied arrangement in the felicitous whole.

They bought it when they moved from England seven years ago. "If we were going to move to New York then Darryl wanted to live in Harlem. I was in England, in not the most creative period of my life, when I saw this boarded-up house on the StreetEasy website. I phoned Darryl and said, 'Go look.'"

What followed was an epic adventure into the wilder shores of house purchase. They had form on rescuing melancholy buildings, having rescued a decaying house near Oxford years before — it became a model of stunning interiors and great gardens. But they had no idea of the nightmare in store for them here.

They are neither of them what you might call entrepreneurs. James Fenton is a major poet of emotional depth and lyric beauty (although his poems occasionally have a refreshing sting of venom), who has lived a wide-ranging life. He has farmed in the Philippines and was a war correspondent in Vietnam, riding the first North Vietnamese tank into the presidential palace when Saigon fell in 1975. He is an acclaimed playwright and has been

The paint has been removed from the carved mahogany of the dining room, but the missing coving on the plaster ceiling has yet to be replaced. This is the first of four oval rooms, where even the windows and the doors are curved.

a political journalist and a drama critic, loves opera, the theater, is a regular book reviewer and columnist (a salient point is that he once wrote a libretto for *Les Misérables* which, although not produced in his version, gave him a share in the proceeds from the subsequent musical). He is also a discerning collector. Darryl Pinckney is an erudite American novelist, dramatist, reviewer and columnist with many awards to his name. He is also a long-time collaborator with the experimental theater director Robert Wilson, and he wrote the scenario for the ballet-drama *Letter to a Man*, with Mikhail Baryshnikov as Nijinsky.

One of James's poems is called "A Vacant Possession" — and the house that Darryl and he uncovered and that is now in their possession was more than vacant: it was screamingly empty, desolate, fought over and beleaguered.

It had been a place of worship for the snappily named Commandment Keepers Ethiopian Hebrew Congregation of the Living God Pillar & Ground of Truth, Inc., who believe that people of Ethiopian descent represent one of the lost tribes of Israel and claim King Solomon and the Queen of Sheba as their

ancestors. Anyway. When the synagogue went on the market a protracted and bitter battle developed between various warring factions of the sect. This was finally resolved in a court judgment, but even then the new owners had to endure barracking, windows being broken and protesters vandalizing the building. "It made life unpleasant," James says. But they faced it down and never lost their passion for the derelict old beauty.

"A year after we had bought it we got our ducks in a row and were able to start work — but every time we arrived the door would be padlocked or we'd find crazy glue on the door. I remember when the removal men first came to deliver stuff we had to guarantee they had come to the right address — they simply could not countenance that anyone lived here."

When they moved in they had three usable rooms — a study each and a bedroom — but no shower and only a makeshift sink. "We showered at the gym and ate out for at least a year . . . we had to upgrade the gas supply, the electrical system, everything. At one time some small-time thief took all the lead from the house. And then we found a gushing great geyser in the basement."

ABOVE The library occupies an extension added in the 1920s. The metal shelving is a classic Dieter Rams design, manufactured by Vitsœ. The print is by Howard Hodgkin. OPPOSITE A glimpse of a green bathroom, off a landing painted in Pacific Ocean Blue (by Benjamin Moore, like nearly all the paints used). Much of the original main staircase had been removed, but here you can see the rich oak panelling and the balusters with their alternating barley-sugar twist. The chest on the landing is made of Italian intarsia work fragments. The bronze head is by Peggy Garland. The painting is Genoese and the marble relief is Paduan. PAGES 210–211 The kitchen stove occupies the space where the original stood, and is surrounded by the original tilework, found under a layer of plaster. The red chairs are Emeco's classic "Navy" chair. To the right of the cooker hangs a Tom Phillips print based on an old postcard. The poster by the window is from an Edinburgh exhibition of daguerreotypes and the photos are mostly by friends. The shelves, from the former Archivia bookshop on Lexington, hold cookbooks.

You have to see this house to believe how immense is the work they have undertaken. Even imagining it makes one want to go and lie down in a darkened room; the fire escapes snaking up the exterior have to be dismantled, and the original delicate ironwork over the oriel-like grids on the windows, the endless railings around the house, all are being scraped down by hand in Sisyphean labor.

When Darryl first went to reconnoiter the building it was in complete darkness and he had to explore the huge interior by the light of a torch, but he telephoned James in astonishment to relay what he was seeing, room by room . . . "and some of them are *oval*!" The idea of oval rooms fascinated them both – and indeed they are beautiful rooms, with their mahogany doors following the curve of the walls. (They later discovered in part of their deep research that the architect, Frank Hill Smith, had previously – in the mid-1880s – built a fine house with oval rooms in Boston.)

Everywhere was neglect and depredation, with the rooms' fine proportions disguised. The second floor had been divided up into many small rooms, and the ghostly shadows of their partitions are still visible – but the plasterwork and fireplaces had not been damaged. The same with the kitchen, where three rented rooms had been squashed into the space and where they found, hidden behind plaster, the original tiles around the cooker.

The house was built in 1890 by John Dwight, a co-founder of Arm & Hammer, a household name still for products such as baking soda and toothpaste (the monogrammed initials JD remain impressed in the plaster on the dining room). Soon after James and Darryl bought it they were delighted to find that the Dwight family still had photographs of the building taken in the 1920s, before they sold it – plus, best of all, the plans and blueprints. Every room save the cellar and bathrooms had been documented. "We were thrilled. We invited them to lunch in their old dining room – we made a camp kitchen, had a cook and a waiter and a three-course meal in the empty building and they didn't bat an eyelid."

Their contractor, Miles Casey, called the Dwight trove "the Rosetta Stone," and architect Sam White, great-grandson of Stanford White, was riveted by the precise documentation. "Before we had the photos, he had made a guess at what the entrance hall would have looked like (based on the earlier house in Boston) but then we found it was a different version of the same idea. Sam played a major role in the early stages, getting the basic things seen to – mostly technical like the redesign of the drainage and the water and so forth." Although they used the invaluable documentation they did not build a simulacrum – as James says, "We are not aiming to take it back to the 1890s but to act freely within the general idiom of the original structure." As a result nearly all the magnificent rooms and landings, so badly treated over the years, have been restored to their previous dignity and first shape and function.

LEFT A small study, painted in glowing Fresh Scent Green. The drawings and prints are by Daumier and others. The filigree stencilled frieze was designed and executed by artist Jane Warrick. The ceilings are painted in the very pale blue Morning Glory, the default color throughout the upper floor. PAGES 214–215 This one of the three oval bedrooms is painted in Smoldering Red, with Paddington Blue for a contrasting trim (imitating the blue of standard painters' masking tape). The matching bedspread is by Missoni. By the window is a plaster bust of an African man, inscribed Kongo. Framed Persian carpet fragments hang on the wall.

ABOVE The yellow drawing room, with its elaborate plaster ceiling painted in White Sand, is restored to its former glory. The fireplace with its onyx surround is original; a small group of Renaissance bronzes and baroque terracotta figures finds its home here, below a fine Regency mirror. The rug is Indian. The architect, Sam White, gave the chandelier as a present to the house. OPPOSITE LEFT The stencilled frieze in blue and Dutch Gold by Jane Warrick pays homage to the long-gone original Lincrusta frieze in green and gold. OPPOSITE RIGHT The restored former servants' staircase has the woodwork painted in Day's End, and the walls in Pacific Ocean Blue.

The detailed carving on the mahogany woodwork, concealed under thick layers of paint, was painstakingly stripped back to crisp detail. The fireplaces, with their elaborate overmantels and surrounds, including Mexican onyx, are in working order, and the kitchen now looks much as it did decades ago. The fine floors, hidden under dingy wall-to-wall carpeting, have been sanded down and strewn with handsome old rugs and carpets that were "mostly cheaply bought at auctions." The panelling, frowsty under its heavy coats of paint, was also stripped down – a time-consuming project – and plaster casts have been made to restore woodcarvings, friezes and pilasters.

When it came to the decoration of the rooms, that was all James's work. Every corner of this massive house speaks of its owners' sensibilities and courage, not to say poetic stoutheartedness.

They aren't only restoring the house. Their lives teem with books, so as well as the library built in 1920 they have added a new one in what used to be a servants' room, using the German classic shelving system designed by Dieter Rams and manufactured by Vitsœ since the 1960s. Other fine bookshelves came from Archivia, a favorite bookshop on Lexington Avenue. "Then one I day I walked past and the shutters were up. I rattled on them and the owner came to the door. She was closing it down. "You can't run a bookshop on the Upper East Side any more." I asked what was going to happen to the shelves and it seemed they were probably going to the dumpster."

Well, here they are now in their alluring new-old library and very fine they are.

And every room resonates with particular glorious color. A central upstairs landing – a room in itself, with its dark blue ceiling and mahogany beams – has *trompe l'œil* porphyria walls and blue stencilled friezes over Dutch Gold, by the artist Jane Warrick. There are two grand pianos in the stunning yellow drawing room, and the back staircase is a shade of indigo that is like a desert sky at night. Every room has its lacings of rare and distinctive objects, the fruits of James's many years as a collector, in an uncommon mixture of exuberance and gravitas, of enjoyment and dignity. "Where do you get all these treasures?" I exclaim; and he admits "I look at catalogues a lot of the time."

On one landing are chairs by Robert Gillow, an English furniture-maker who started out as a carpenter on a ship bound for the West Indies in 1720. There he became interested in mahogany and brought samples of the wood back (the first mahogany to be imported to England) and in 1730 he founded a firm, Gillow of Lancaster, which supplied quality furniture and furnishings to the English gentry. James has had them covered in a Bhutanese fabric he found in Robert Kime's enticing shop in London.

The undertaking of the rebuilding of this historically important mansion has become a much bigger and more expensive endeavor than they envisaged – almost a chivalric venture. The work continues year by year and as they research and restore they discover new things all the time about American furniture and interiors.

They have created something which reflects the original grandeur of the house but which is also of their own time, and reflects their sensibility and their poetic and artistic occupations. They both know that without their rescue this stately grande dame of a house would have been gutted or even demolished. And they get great satisfaction from seeing the house come alive and breathe again. And they love living there.

INDEX

Page numbers in *italic* refer to captions.